A Fresh Challenge

A Fresh Challenge

by Bert Houghton

ISBN 0 9514193 3 1

Front cover photograph:
The coastal path as it approaches Kellan Head, North Cornwall

Produced through MRM Associates Ltd.,
Unit C4, Weldale Street, Reading, Berks RG1 7BX

Foreword

In the early 1980's my heart was causing me mobility problems. My wife was pushing me around in a wheel-chair more frequently, I could not climb the stairs and not walk more than a few yards on level ground. I was given the chance to have a triple heart by-pass operation and afterwards set myself the challenge to walk the South West Coastal Path. I realised this would include several steep gradients such as Golden Cap and Black Ven on the Dorset coastline and the Great Hangman on Devon's North Coast.

My purpose in writing this book is to encourage people with similar disabilities and to show them that they still have a worthwhile future ahead of them.

ACKNOWLEDGEMENTS
I would like to express my thanks to all those who have helped me –
Mr Treasure – the surgeon and his devoted team at The Middlesex Hospital
My Step-son Bill Fiddler and his wife Maree
My Step-daughter Sue Bourne and her husband Roger
My Grandaughter Catherine
My Canadian cousin Dianne Scoles
and finally
My wife Ruth for her company and continuous encouragement, especially on some of the toughest parts of our walk, when I was ready to give up.

Ruth, Tina and myself, Swanage seafront at the end of day one

The South West Coastal Path
A Fresh Challenge

There was no doubt that my old pump was in urgent need of repair. After many visits to hospital for various tests, some of which were rather unpleasant, the specialist came to the conclusion that over the years high living on fat beef, pork and lamb, too many bacon and egg breakfasts and lavish helpings of home produced butter and cream had caused trouble in the works.

Consequently at the Middlesex Hospital on a bright spring morning in March 1985 Mr Treasure, a very skilful surgeon and his devoted team performed open heart surgery on my failing ticker. Removing a vein from my left leg from ankle to knee which I was assured could be spared without ill effect, it was turned inside out, cleaned and used to patch up the faulty heart arteries. I realise that this is very much a layman's description of events for what appears in reality to be a very skilful and delicate operation, but thankfully it did return me to good health once more, all this I must add free of charge to myself on the wonderful national health service.

A few days after leaving the intensive care unit the physiotherapist had me climbing two flights of stairs and disregarding the hospital's efficient lifts.

After giving me the all clear, my surgeon's advice was to take up walking on a serious scale, at least three or four miles each day, and whilst I wouldn't be placed on a strict diet common sense should prevail, I should eat more sensibly in future. In a way this was a second lease of life, another bite of the apple so to speak. Not a person to do things by half I made a decision to seek out some tough new challenge. I would attempt to walk Britain's longest footpath and although many dream of the feat, few achieve it.

There can be no better way to experience the diverse coastline and ever-changing landscapes of the Southwest peninsular than to walk the coastal path, well clear of the rat race, rushing traffic and the bustle of holidaymakers. The wild rocky coastline, isolated coves, long beaches and quaint fishing villages, none of which can be seen at their best from a motorcar.

The Southwest way is by far the longest of the official long distance trails, it runs from South Haven Point on the South side of Poole Harbour in Dorset right round the Southwest peninsular via Lands End to Minehead in Somerset. The experts reckon this path is 594 miles long or thereabouts, others differ on the mileage but all agree, including my wife Ruth and myself it is a fair old step!! So come now with me in your minds eye and walk the path which was once the patrol area of coastguards on the lookout for smugglers and invaders. But tread carefully there is always danger for the unwary.

Ruth and I had planned to walk the coastal path joining up each section on different days. We would not miss out any of the walk even if it meant a tramp through built up or uninteresting areas, or a long diversion inland to negotiate some water obstacle.

Although now reasonable fit our age barred us from the rigors of humping a back pack complete with sleeping bag and all the necessary gear. We have a serviceable but rather old fashioned tent which we pitched on suitable sites near the section of the path to be walked. From these base camps we either made use of the local bus service or failing that, in isolated areas hired a taxi to take us some ten or twelve miles down the coast to walk back to join the spot were the previous days hike had ended. By this leap frog method we could travel very light and carry the minimum of food and water as we found that on a long strenuous walk all we needed in the way of refreshment was a cold lemon drink, a sandwich or two and a bar of chocolate. Usually after a fifteen minute break we were once again eager to press on. As for our dog Tina, who was our constant companion for most of the walk, she detested any prolonged stop and was soon giving a yap or two. This was her way of telling us, 'Come on let's be off.'

Regarding our equipment, when it did rain our good quality breathable waterproofs made an enormous difference to the enjoyment of our walking. At first sight such gear may appear an expensive luxury but having bought it we never again had to worry about a rainy day. Although much cheaper, plastic waterproofs can be extremely sweaty and uncomfortable when you are fighting your way from sea level to the top of a five hundred foot cliff during a sudden downpour, or, worse still, when it decides to rain all day! Some of our walking has been done in trainers during the dry periods, but leather walking boots with commando style grips are much better. They certainly prevented us from slipping on steep slopes, making our walking easier as well as safer.

Our First Day
15th June 1990
South Haven Point Poole to Peveril Point Swanage – 7.5 miles

Note: the distance given in miles between place names is approximate only and via the coastal path.

Poole, the largest town in Dorset with much character and a long history. The almost land locked harbour is ideal for sailing. Its shores, with many beautiful creeks and inlets, measure nearly one hundred miles. Near the entrance lies five hundred acre Brownsea Island a wildlife sanctuary. Just across that narrow strip of water is South Haven Point and it was here on an overcast, but mild June morning that Ruth and I started our walk of the

Sandbanks. The start of the coastal walk

Southwest coastal path. The question was would we ever get to Minehead? This first section of the path follows the natural curve of Shell Bay and for almost three miles it's hard going walking on soft sand. On the landward side is Studland Heath National Nature Reserve, a bird watchers paradise. We spent some time watching the many and varied water birds in this quiet isolated area. A large freshwater lake called Little Sea is home for many rare species including all six British reptiles. Further on, one section of this long beach is reserved for nude bathing and one is warned in good time by a prominent sign to that effect, but at that early hour we saw only one lonely mortal braving the elements.

The path which continues round Studland Bay now turns almost due South atop the white chalk cliffs to The Foreland. It was 11 am when we got to this beautiful spot, we took the opportunity to sit on the downland grass for a well earned snack and admire the scene. There in the sea just out from the shore

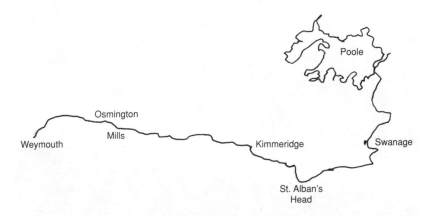

Poole

Osmington
Mills

Weymouth

Kimmeridge

Swanage

St. Alban's
Head

stands the Devil's Stacks. Dramatic chalk pillars which include Old Harry and the slender Old Harry's wife, both being gradually eroded by the waves. Turning almost back on itself the path now traverses 'Old Nick's ground.' (I wonder who he was, quite a character no doubt!) Keeping to the high ground, in no time at all we were walking above the chalk cliffs of the Pinnacles, typical of the scenery to be found on this coastline. With few humans around to disturb the peace there is an abundance of sea birds in this area. Cormorants stood motionless on offshore rocks, wings outstretched drying themselves in the sunshine. Parent seagulls swoop, dive and call incessantly drawing our attention away from their young perched precariously on narrow ledges hundreds of feet above the crashing waves below, and there were some nests with young cormorants which even as we watched were being fed by their parent birds with fish plucked from the sea.

Now the path rises up to the high point of Ballard Cliff. Ruth found the going tough so we sat for a while taking in the marvellous view of Swanage across the bay. At the western end of the cliff the path now drops rapidly to the sandy beach. After a while it swings inland to a built-up area and it was not long before we were hopelessly lost amongst the side streets. However, a local lady kindly offered to walk with us, taking us to the beach and back on course once more, but before setting off again we sat on

Ballard Point and the Chalk Stacks of Old Harry

the seafront and enjoyed a 50p ice-cream. With everyone else clad in bright summer dresses, shorts or scanty swimsuits we got the impression that we looked an odd pair dressed in our waterproofs, heavy hiking boots, and back packs. Swinging a walking stick each and a springer spaniel trailing behind us! It is quite a step along Swanage seafront past the pier, the lifeboat house and finally out to the lookout post on Peveril Point where we decide to call it a day.

16th June 1990
Worth Matravers to Peveril Point – 4.5 miles

At this stage of our walk we had pitched our tent at Ulwell Cottage caravan park. The following day a short car journey took us to Worth Matravers, an idyllic spot with cottages built of grey

Purbeck stone and a central village pond which gives Worth Matravers an atmosphere of tranquillity. I noticed one cottage is named after Isaac Gulliver, an eighteenth century smuggler who was revered as a hero by the locals and who shared in his spoils. Although a mile or so from the beach this village is a good starting point for walking along an excellent stretch of the coastal path. We followed a well marked footpath down hill all the way to Seacombe Cliff before turning eastwards this time. The path often runs close to the cliff edge and is hazardous in windy conditions, however we made it safely to Dancing Ledge with its small swimming pool cut into the rocks by quarrymen at the beginning of this century. The Purbeck stone quarried at this isolated spot was once shipped out in flat bottomed boats to a waiting ketch, but those days are long gone. At one point looking down from the high cliff one can see a large cannon. This was swept from the ship, the Halsewell which was caught in a violent storm and destroyed at Halsewell Bars in 1786. It is reported that one hundred and sixty six people died including the captain and his two daughters.

By twelve noon we had reached Anvil Point and the lighthouse, what better spot to enjoy some light refreshment. Chicken sandwiches, an apple and a drink of lemon juice from our meagre rations. We have long discovered that it is unwise to indulge in too much food and drink with still a long strenuous walk in front of us, nor lay out in the sun and fall asleep. If you do, it's just impossible to coax old legs into action again. The path now follows very close to the cliffs giving splendid views of the seabirds milling below. I couldn't help but smile at the sign I noticed on the very edge of a particular cliff top. It read:- TO LET. "SEACLIFFS" a desirable high rise residence, with extensive sea views, offering these superb advantages; Safe and predator proof, easy take off and landing, two minutes flight time from food supply. A wide variety of ledges and nest holes available. We follow these cliffs around Durlston Bay through dense and mature woodland consisting mainly of Holm Oaks, passing to the seaward side of most of the buildings. This clifftop route soon emerges on the green areas of Peveril Point. We had completed another interesting section of the path.

17th June 1990
Kimmeridge to Worth Matravers – 6.5 miles

Kimmeridge. On the low unstable cliffs is a nodding donkey. It bobs at the head of a well where oil was discovered in 1958 at a depth of one thousand eight hundred feet and produces about one and a half million gallons of oil per year. Whilst these pumps are a common sight in the States, Canada and many other parts of the world they are a rare sight on mainland Britain. From the oil well the path keeps to the clifftop, passes to the seaward side of a row of cottages at Gaulter Gap, and then makes for Clavel Tower at the eastern end of the bay. The weather on this particular morning was dull and overcast with a certain amount of sea mist drifting in from the coast. I was not optimistic of seeing much sun. After breakfast at our camp site we drove down to Worth Matravers. I had telephoned for a taxi to collect Ruth and me at 10 am where we had agreed we would await its arrival at the duck pond. The driver arrived on the dot. Putting our walking gear, sandwiches etc. in the taxi cab boot he drove us to Kimmeridge dropping us off at the toll gate which was as far as he could go. The cost of this twenty five minute drive through the beautiful Dorset countryside was £12.50. I gave him £1.50 tip as he had been very helpful with directions and suggestions for our marathon walk along the coast path back to Seacombe Cliff, and inland to Worth Matravers a journey that was to take over six hours of hard strenuous walking, particularly the ascent of the five hundred foot Houns-tout cliff. We had lumbered badly out of puff up this ferociously steep hill, but once on the top, the view is stunning. Ahead whaleback hills and radiant white cliffs. Houns-tout is a very distinctive peak, capped with limestone, which is porous. This means that water which falls on top of the limestone filters through to the Kimmeridge shales below, which gradually, after becoming saturated turn into a porridge – like mess. From time to time these black layers flow out from under the limestone leaving it without support, and thousands of tons of rock cascade down into the sea. The very severe drop to Chapman's Pool needs very careful walking before the path swings inland to the small settlement of

The cliffs of Swyre Head. Ruth and Tina contemplate the climb ahead

Hill Bottom. We sat on a small brick built bridge to eat a quick lunch, unfortunately the weather deteriorated at this point and we had to don our waterproofs which didn't help us to conquer yet another cliff, the huge limestone face of Emmett's Hill. Some of the cliff climbs make the ascent of Beacon Hill back near our home in Berkshire seem like a gentle uphill stroll! On the summit the royal marines have recently completed a picnic table with seats constructed of marble. Built and opened to the public June 1st 1990 it overlooks Emmett's Hill and Chapman's Pool and it is in memory of the Deal Disaster.

Once on the high plateau, apart from a dip here and there the path keeps to the cliff top all the way to St Aldhelm's or St Alban's head. St Aldhelm was a Saxon bishop of Sherborne, born before the middle of the seventh century he founded the monasteries at Frome in Somerset and Bradford-on-Avon in Wiltshire. It had been an arduous climb to reach the top of this peninsular and we rested there for some time, no doubt because of its isolation the wildlife there is quite outstanding. Puffins, Razorbills, and Guillemots nest on the narrow ledges of these cliffs and rear their young, leaving again in late May or early June for a lonely life many miles out to sea. We also saw Shags, Cormorants, Kittiwakes, Fulmers and Black-headed Gulls. The National Trust owns substantial stretches of these cliffs and manages the clifftop meadows in order to protect the rare flora. At the time of year Ruth and I walked this section of the path it really was very beautiful. In passing I noticed that the grazing sheep were not short of grass despite the fact that the farming tenants are restricted in the use of fertilisers and chemical sprays.

At St Aldelm's Head you leave behind the magnificent views of Weymouth Bay, the white chalk cliffs of Purbeck and the black cliffs of Kimmeridge shales and once around the headland on a clear day one can see the Isle of Wight. A mile west of St Aldelm's Head our route turned, going about a hundred yards inland before descending steeply through a thicket to the Winspit Valley. Winspit is a group of cliff quarries apparently last worked during the Second World War. The path rises behind the quarries and stays on the cliff top until descending once again to Seacombe

Bottom. A detour is made round the back of more quarries then from the back of Seacombe Cliff the path strikes east along the cliff top. From now on we had no problem on a mostly down hill section to return to the previous days starting point. Today has been a hard walk but very rewarding and well worth the effort involved.

18th June 1990
Osmington Mills to Kimmeridge – 15 miles

Awoke to a steady downpour. Life under canvas is fun in fine, sunny weather but nothing is more disheartening than trying to cook breakfast with a southwest gale threatening to blow your tent into the sea at any moment, and the rain drips down your neck as you crouch over a primus stove trying your best to warm up a tin of soup and at the same time drum up some enthusiasm for this open air life! Enough is enough, summer weather had got the better of us, we decided to break camp, move on and find shelter for a night or two to give us the opportunity to dry out and recharge the batteries, so to speak. Packing everything into the car we drove westwards along deserted Dorset lanes. The high ground above Lulworth Camp was sheathed in clouds and still the rain poured down. A soldier on guard duty turned us back with the explanation that the army was about to fire a "Viper" whatever that maybe!

At West Lulworth we booked in at a comfortable homely bed and breakfast establishment. The landlady had a son that ran a taxi service very convenient for our needs, and the next morning he drove Ruth, Tina and myself to Osmington Mills. Access to the coast path here is through the car park of the thirteenth century thatched smugglers inn. Going east the path runs almost past the front door of the pub, no doubt the landlord had had a say in planning this route! Despite the fact that we hadn't yet worked up a thirst we couldn't resist the temptation to nip in for a quick one. Leaving the pub the path now skirts round the landward side of the bar, by the old coastguard cottages then after a stiff climb one stays to the seaward side of a large field, over a stile then keeps to the clifftop for a further one and a half miles. Just beyond the modern settlement of Ringstead village there is a field enclosed on all sides by woods. This is the site of the deserted medieval village of Ringstead. Local legend has it that French pirates burnt the village, killed the male inhabitants, and made off with the women. Another reason for desertion could have been the Black Death, or, more than likely because of economic and agricultural changes that destroyed the livelihood of the population.

The path now passes inland, past a caravan site then goes through an area of thicket to emerge beside Burning Cliff so called because in 1826 chemical reactions in the rock ignited the oil rich shales. We now followed the track east through the 115 acre Dorset Trust Nature Reserve of small valleys and dense undergrowth, it is the home of many rare plants, butterflies and birds and we dawdled long in this beautiful spot. We continued on our way to the chapel of St Catherine's, three miles from this point, staying on the clifftop all the way one now arrives at Durdle Door one of the most famous landmarks on the south coast of England. The spectacular natural arch of Portland limestone sculpted by the sea. The final approach to this arch is by a flight of steps which runs down to this beautiful isolated cove and its crystal clear water, well worth the extra steps. Just before reaching Durdle Door I trained my binoculars on four rocks lying offshore simply to try to deduce how they came by their names. The Cow, The Blind Cow, The Bull and of course The Calf, for the life of me I could not see that they remotely resembled the shape of these animals, did some long dead farmer name them in memory of his small herd of cattle swept out to sea in a violent winter storm?

Meanwhile, heading east, the coast path stays on top of the cliff rising to Hambury Tout. Below there are dramatic multi – coloured chalk cliffs and looking back one gets an excellent view of Bat's Head, White Nothe, the whole of Weymouth Bay and the Isle of Portland. At this point Lulworth Cove and the Royal Armoured Corps gunnery range comes into sight. The range which covers more than seven thousand acres can be crossed by a series of marked paths when tanks are not firing. On the day that Ruth and I passed through we were diverted far inland by soldiers on sentry duty. Although the tanks were not in action small arms fire was keeping up a regular tattoo, not only disturbing the peacefulness of the area, but adding some three miles to our day's walk! On this day we had made an early start yet it was six thirty pm before footsore and weary we completed this onerous section of the path. The scenery had been out of this world, rugged cliffs and lonely beaches that are inaccessible except on foot or by boat. Just ourselves, the views and the elements.

19th June 1990
Osmington Mills to Weymouth – 6 miles

We spent another night at Elads-Nevar, West Road, West Lulworth. Very hospitable with a first class English breakfast all for the cost of eleven pounds each. About 9 am we drove into Weymouth leaving the car in the car park near the Overcombe Shell garage. We rang for a taxi which was with us in three minutes flat. Clad in full walking gear, our rucksacks stuffed with our waterproofs, camera, light refreshments and our ordnance survey map and a very excited springer spaniel, no doubt thinking to herself: 'What some people do for fun.' The driver took us to Osmington Mills. The weather at that point in time was warm and sunny, but a gale force wind was to blow all day and since on this occasion we were walking westwards into the wind it added to the energy required to ascend high cliffs, but luckily the gradients on the path in this area are not too severe. At Black Head just west of Osmington Mills a recent, extremely large landslide has swept away the coast path which necessitated a wide detour inland adding perhaps two miles to our planned mileage for the day. Back onto the normal path once more we rounded Redcliff Point and now crossed the broad expanse of green turf on Furzy Cliff, an ideal spot for picnics, but that is for people with time to spare.

Bowleaze Cove was below us with its beach of sand, shingle and

17

small seaweed covered rocks. A pretty spot where the promenade and long sandy beach beckoned (but unfortunately we could not pause). By four o'clock in the afternoon we were striding confidently along the seafront of the fashionable resort of Weymouth.

Later that evening we struggled to pitch our tent in a gale force wind. Until one has succeeded in hammering the last tent peg home one's night time shelter is in imminent danger of vanishing into the sea or the next county. Luckily the wind abated during the night and the next day broke bright and clear.

20th June 1990
Weymouth to Abbotsbury via Western Ledges and Portland Harbour – 10 miles

The 20th June only 24 hours short of the years longest daylight hours and we had planned to walk the nine mile long Chesil Beach, not an easy task by any means. One doesn't walk on the billions of pebbles which form this immense bank of shingle but one follows the coastline of the East Fleet and West Fleet, the seven mile long lagoon behind the beach. If one cares to look at an ordnance survey of the area you will notice that the coastal path closely follows every bend and curve and at times goes far inland, a route so tortuous that it looks for all the world like the outline of a jigsaw piece, which must almost double the mileage of walking this section. This stretch of the path is difficult to negotiate, mainly due to the military installations and the danger areas. The first obstacle of this nature is the Royal Engineers Bridging Camp which has to be passed on the landward side. The army has provided a fenced footpath all the way round the camp which adds some two miles to the walk. Further on one enters Littlesea Holiday Park, passing to the seaward side of the massed ranks of caravans. Not my idea of a holiday, the communal life with crowded camp shops, pet dogs and packed humanity on the beaches. For my choice give me the solitude of the uninhabited

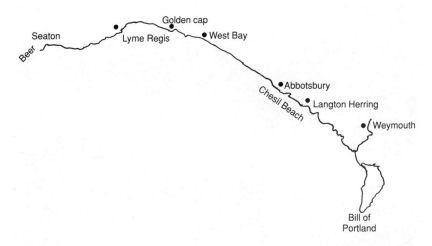

rugged coast line and the lonely clifftop downland anytime. Shortly after this we came to the Chickerell rifle range at Tidmoor Point. The red flags were flying, an indication that firing was taking place. A sentry posted on the outskirts of the range escorted us across when it was safe to do so. South of the village of Langton Herring the path strikes far inland and from an high ridge we could look down on the unique Abbottsbury Swannery where up to 500 mute swans may be seen in summer. Apparently this number increases to nearly a thousand in the winter months. It is the only nesting colony of mute swans in Britain and dates from the 11th century when Benedictine Monks of Abbottsbury reared the birds for meat. Time didn't allow us to actually visit the Swannery much as we would have liked. It was 6.15 pm when we finally reached the huge tithe barn at Abbottsbury, we had been walking for eight hours and in all that time apart from the army personnel and holidaymakers at the caravan site we hadn't past or met a single person all day.

Early morning breakfast

23rd July 1990
Abbottsbury to West Bay – 9 miles

Left our home in Beautiful Royal Berkshire at 10 am (two hours later than planned) in our red Peugeot 205 to drive to the caravan and tenting camp site at Lower Eype. £6.50 per night. Our tent pitched almost on the cliff edge looked out to sea, just fine unless a gale gets up overnight!! We sat outside our small canvass abode, licking our greasy fingers from our fish and chips purchased at the camp's take-away as darkness fell. Whilst far out to sea, the lights of passing ships bobbed and blinked in the dusky light. The world, or at least this little corner of it, seemed a good and peaceful place.

6am. On Tuesday morning. Sun already high in the sky with all signs of a hot summer's day, breakfast on cornflakes drowned in fresh milk brought from our own farm, these supplies should last us three days if kept in our cold box. Drove our car to West Bay, parked it in the Harbour car park for seven hours at thirty pence per hour. Then caught the bus in the square at the front of the George Hotel. £1 each to Abbottsbury. We thoroughly enjoyed a pleasant bus ride through Dorset countryside. This in itself can be quite an interesting experience, the little 16 seater trundles around narrow high banked lanes, the driver, often female, follows the prescribed tortuous route from one isolated village community to the next, collecting buxom country ladies making for the nearest town shop and a few elderly pensioners on the weekly excursion to collect their State hand-out. OK, I do the same, how else could I pay for this bus ride? A pair of strange faces usually draws attention especially if the owners are dressed in hiking gear, are humping a couple of rucksacks and have a dog in tow. Ruth and I usually pass the time of day and get into conversation with them. One gets the impression that the locals in the depth of these rural areas have not so far been invaded by the swarms of holidaymakers who usually make for the largest seaside caravan site.

We left the bus at Abbottsbury with a cheery wave to our route companions of the last forty minutes or so and set off down a narrow lane to pick up the coastal path once more. Although we hadn't done any coastal path walking for more than a month Ruth and I were in fine fettle. Which was just as well because we still had a fair stretch of Chesil Beach to walk and although it is straight and level it is very hard going, walking on the loose pebbles often ankle deep in places, two steps forward and one back! Generations of experts on geology have failed to work out how the billions of pebbles which form this immense bank of shingle are graded from west to east, becoming bigger and bigger towards the Isle of Portland. What we did discover was that the smaller the stones the harder forward progress became. At last onto firmer ground as we reached Burton road really no more than a rough gravel track. Past the 'Old Coast Guards' which is the name of a row of wooden clad cottages, now modernised and looking quite respectable, whilst just across a field on the crest of a small rise lies a lonely farm house and cluster of buildings. You are looking at "Labour in Vain Farm." There have been plenty of times in the past that I have thought that our own Mousefield Farm could have justified such a name! Adjacent to West Bexington just off the track itself was a large gathering of hippies or new age travellers as they are now known with their collection of old buses, furniture vans, clapped out cars, children and Alsation dogs they where indeed a most unsavoury crowd. Ruth and I quickened our steps and were pleased to leave them behind us. We were now on Cogden Beach which is of course part of Chesil Beach. The official route of the coastal path passes to the landward side of a lake called Burton Mere but this can be difficult and often wet so we chose to walk on the seaward side of it. Finally, leaving the mountain of pebbles behind us we reached the Old Coastguards caravan site, here one has to make way through as best one can, then climb to the top of Burton Cliff for a while until reaching the river Bride where we were compelled to follow the river upstream for some distance to cross by way of a footbridge. The path now ascends to the top of East Cliff running alongside the golf links and giving excellent views across Lyme Bay. Our days walk ended at West Bay or Bridport Harbour as it used to be known in days gone by.

Ruth and I have a passion for poring over the minutiae of maps which is perhaps understandable since local knowledge prior to a walk is important. We get a lot of enjoyment from this detailed route planning which is often done during long winter evenings in the comfort of our lounge, sitting in front of a huge log fire surrounded by acres of ordnance survey maps. On the walk itself one cannot of course do much about the weather, you can take precaution against the cold and wet, but there is nothing you can do about the wind except try to avoid it, or get the right side of it! However with the wind behind me I hope to keep walking into the 21st century.

24th July 1990
Eype (West Bay) to Lyme Regis – 8 miles
According to the weather report we are all set for a very warm, sultry day

Ruth and I planned to continue our coastal walk setting off from our camp site at Eype. The stint to Lyme Regis a distance of about 8 miles would include some of the toughest stretches so far. We had to conquer the 626 foot summit of Golden Cap the highest cliff in southern England. Away to an early start at 6.30 am before it got too hot, a well marked path on the top of West Cliff leads past some limestone workings and the ruins of a lime kiln, before dropping down to cross Eype Mouth by the stepping stones next to lobster pots and fishing boats. Now one is faced by a strenuous climb to reach Thorncombe Beacon but once at the top the views are magnificent, and continue so as you pass just behind Doghouse Hill and around Ridge Cliff before dropping down to Seatown; a pretty village with thatched cottages of honey coloured stone and a beach of golden shingle which shelves steeply above low tide sand. We passed over the small river by going inland a short distance and across the bridge. Leaving Seatown the path swings inland crossing meadows knee deep in grass waiting for a settled spell and the farmer's mower. Climbing steadily south of Langdon Hill we decided to take a refreshment stop before attempting the more severe gradients ahead. The path now zigzags upwards through a wooded section, next across a steep incline covered in clumps of bright yellow gorse until finally we are on the golden sandstone summit of Golden Cap. With this climb behind us what else can the path throw up that can prevent this pair of old age pensioners from reaching Lands End just a mere 277 miles around the zigzagged coast line.

Just west of Golden Cap the path drops down to a small hollow, crosses a bridge and then rises once again to regain the next high point. Most of the land in this area is owned by the National Trust which ensures that the route is kept open when another chunk of land is claimed by the sea. Approaching Westhay Farm the path keeps straight ahead before dropping down to the lower cliffs where it clings precariously to the seaward edge of the field then swings inland around Cain's Folly staying on the cliff top until descending to cross the River Char which trickles into the sea over the sandy beach. I could not help but reminisce that the last time I was at Charmouth was way back in the distant past when as a young lad I was treated to a rare day out at the seaside by my late Uncle Sid and Aunt Dorie who lived and farmed at School House Farm, Sadborrow. On this visit today I spent just one hour browsing through the information barn and museum with its large collection of fossilised marine creatures, the remains of animals that lived some 200 million years ago, when this area was under the sea.

Landslides occur between Lyme and Charmouth without warning and as we climbed upwards towards the top of Black Ven the path was closed for that very reason and we were diverted far inland to skirt The Spitties a vast area of unstable land, quicksands and bog. Safely around this obstacle we dropped down, down, down through the dense woodland to arrive at Lyme Regis by 3 pm, where we spent an hour on the stony beach cooling our blistered feet in the sea.

25th July 1990
Beer to Lyme Regis – 8 miles

Another warm, cloudless day was forecast although visibility out to sea was limited somewhat. We left our camp site at 8.10 am and drove to Lyme Regis where we left our car on the outskirts of town in the long stay car park, for just seventy pence all day. We walked back to the Square and sat on the sea front for a while before catching a 9.22 am bus for Beer. On arrival we walked down Beer's main street, alongside a trickling stream which slopes down to a shingle beach sheltered by high cliffs of crumbling chalk. No time was wasted in the town, it is eight miles by coastal path to Lyme Regis. Above the beach and opposite the Anchor Inn the path starts more or less on a level course on the clifftop overlooking ranks of fishing boats pulled up on the pebbles below. After about five hundred yards a steep flight of concrete steps leads into a narrow lane then down to a post box and telephone kiosk at Seaton Hole. Now we followed the old Beer road towards the sea front at Seaton. We don't enjoy walking the esplanade of seaside towns with their ranks of small hotels and Guest houses, but I am not one to miss out busy built up areas as it is all part of the walk. Upon reaching the river Axe we crossed over on the new concrete bridge which was under construction at the time.

Just north of the bridge is a sign 'Welcome to Axe Bridge Golf Club' and here the coast path follows a shaded, narrow lane overhung with a mass of honeysuckle and broom until reaching the club house. One has to walk through the golf course following little white sign posts straight up the valley until coming to a stile with fine views back towards Beer Head. After crossing a number of fields you enter the National Nature Reserve and it is worthwhile to remember that once you enter this reserve it is six miles to the other end and since the path passes through jungle like woodland for the whole way walking can be very demanding, especially if it has been raining recently when the path will be slippery on the steeper slopes. Another point to remember is that once you enter the reserve, the only way out is to give up and retreat, or continue onwards to Lyme Regis, there are no public access points along the way and it becomes impossible to leave the path. These undercliffs are one of the wildest and isolated stretches of coast line in the south of England with high cliffs and constant land movements. The largest land slip took place on Christmas Day 1839 when eight million tons of water logged chalk slipped to create Goat Island. The path twists and turns endlessly, up and down and occasionally almost reverses on itself. At times you dive into dense dark green undergrowth where the sun rarely filters through and the sky is only seen in glimpses through the canopy above. Without warning you break into a clearing beneath tall ash and sycamore trees with their trunks draped in ivy and from the branches hang such vast tangles of vines and creepers that one almost expects Tarzan of the Apes to come swinging through the air with mind chilling whoops. The path begins to go up and down again, and in another half hour we were roughly at the half way point marked by the ruins of an old pumping station. The path now follows the track over a bridge before branching seaward to mount a long flight of wooden steps upwards through a tunnel of hawthorn and hazel, to emerge on a small peak overlooking Charton Bay. The route at Whitlands Cliff is narrow and clings to the side of a steep slope overlooking a deep chasm full of bracken and Hart's Tongue fern. Now moving back from the sea we get a glimpse of the enormous land slip which occurred in 1840 at Humble Green, from now on the view opens up and we walked through an area where the trees lie twisted and broken like matchsticks with a clear swathe right down to the sea, no doubt the aftermath of the 1987 gales. We continued to meander up and down for some miles until finally reaching the eastern boundary of the Nature Reserve, to cross open meadows and a small stream before emerging at the bowling green beside The Cobb. The harbour of Lyme. Because of the dense undergrowth and difficult conditions we had been on the move for seven hours one of the most tiring sections to date.

21st September 1990
Beer to Sidmouth – 9 miles

Unfortunately we cannot continue walking the coastal path on an uninterrupted basis, simply because we have other commitments back at the farm, hence the gaps in the time between each section, although we did religiously continue where we left off on the last walking holiday.

This time picking up the path once more from Beer, having arrived there by local bus from our camp site above Seacombe. On the beach fishermen were busy sorting out their nets, lobster pots and other gear ready for yet another day at sea. Often I find time to chat with the locals but on this day we had set ourselves quite a long stint hoping to get as far as Sidmouth where we had left our

car. Please note if the reader ever tries this section there are quite a number of considerable ascents and descents and it is wise not to judge the effort required purely on the mileage, also there are one or two places in this stretch where it is easy to come off the official route and whilst one is not likely to come to any severe harm it is easy to get lost.

The cliff top walk to Beer Head is well worthwhile and from this high vantage point one gets a marvellous view eastwards round the whole of Seaton Bay. We continued westwards on the high cliffs until first dropping down to Branscombe Mouth then up again keeping high on Coxe's Cliff and Weston Cliff. Now down a long flight of steps to sea level at Weston Combe, a beautiful valley of flowers. As an added bonus a stream races down this grassy ravine before filtering into the sea through a long beach of smooth shingle. Old man's beard, honeysuckle and ivy cling to ancient lichen clad trees and giant slabs of chalk that have fallen from the cliffs over the centuries. There were bramble thickets loaded with tempting ripe black-berries and masses of sloes all of which were unlikely to be gathered, so isolated is this area from civilisation. To continue westwards there is only one way out of this valley and that is by rescue helicopter or on foot climbing endless steps first to the top of Dunscombe Cliff then a few miles further on Salcombe Hill Cliff. This part of the coast is pitted with caves, many of which were once used by smugglers to hide tobacco, brandy and other contraband, but these days modern contrabandist bring in drugs in an unlimited variety of diverse ways. Finally we arrived at Sidmouth but before reaching the esplanade it was necessary to divert inland to cross over the river Sid. It had been a grand walk but we were rather weary to say the least.

22nd September 1990
Exmouth to Sidmouth – 13 miles

Departed from campsite at 8.15 am driving our car to Sidmouth. After parking the car for the day we walked to the Triangle and caught the Devon General 57 bus for Exmouth where we arrived at 10.00am. After a pleasant early morning ride through several picturesque villages, in which the bus swayed down winding lanes and clattered through overhanging branches in a most exciting way. The weather forecast was not hopeful and already there appeared to be many squally showers on the horizon, but luckily at this point in time all were on the far side of the Exe. Our dog Tina was very tired from the previous day's walk and I just hoped she would cope with today's stint of thirteen miles of coastal path walking, not to mention ourselves getting fagged out! Setting out from Exmouth we made for the cliffs at the eastern end of the esplanade. At the far side of the Maer is a recreation ground and here the road forks enclosing a car park, toilets and a cafe. Keeping to the landward side of this car park we turned into Foxholes Hill and now the coastal path stays high all the way to Budleigh Salterton. Two miles out of Exmouth there is a Royal Marine firing range on the seaward side. During our passage through, the peace of Devon was continuously being shattered by rapid small arms fire, but there, I suppose the military have got to get in practice sometime. Once safely on our way the path rises again before dropping briefly through a small valley only to rise again to 'The Floors.' This struck me as a strange name to give to these crumbling cliffs but no doubt there is a very good reason for the appellation.

At Budleigh Salterton, after walking along the front we had to make a detour three quarters of a mile up the river Otter in order to cross on a dyke built by Napoleonic prisoners of war. On the bank of this river is the nature reserve of the Devon Wildlife Trust and we stopped for a while taking shelter in a hide constructed solely for the purpose of watching the many and varied bird life of the area. Continuing along the clifftop the path crosses a large field, then over a stile at the eastern end you join a small lane leading down to Ladram Bay which has a shingle beach, red sandstone stacks and many small caves. We stopped at this point for our lunch break having this quiet spot to ourselves which is not surprising because apart from the village of Otterton and a small caravan site it is a long way from civilisation. I object to a stiff climb straight after lunch but often there is no escape, like today ahead lay Hern Point Rock and the ascent to High Peak but the fine views of Lyme Bay make it well worthwhile. Shortly we entered a small plantation in which lies an Iron Age Fort, the track now meanders through woods just inland of High Peak, continues along the cliff top to Peak Hill and at last we were looking down on the sea front at Sidmouth. I love this little Regency Town, protected on all but the seaward side. Woods and small Devon fields climb the slopes behind the town, other hills, many densely wooded, rise far inland, and to delight the eye is the valley of the river Sid, a brown moorland stream which disappears in shingle on reaching the beach. Huge cliffs drop almost sheer, stretch readily to the east until they change to the white chalk of the Dorset coast, whilst westwards there is a mile long beach below Peak Hill, where at low tide the sweep of the sand changes from pink to gold as it goes further west. At the expense of numerous painful blisters on our feet quite a chunk of the south Devon coast had today been crossed off our maps. The time was 5.30pm. It had taken us seven and a half hours.

23rd September 1990
Maidencombe to Dawlish Warren – 15 miles

We were now faced with that great barrier to anyone on foot, the estuary of the River Exe. There is a passenger ferry in summer but we took the easy way out and drove our car inland to Exeter crossing the river by the M5 motorway toll bridge (toll eastward only). Once on the western side of the river we swung south and pitched our little blue tent at the Holimarine camp site. We were now all set to tackle the next section of the path. Maidencombe to Dawlish Warren, approximately fifteen miles by coastal path which includes yet another water barrier, the River Teign and only once before had we attempted 15 miles. Fully equipped for a long walk which included maps, compass, binoculars, food and ample liquid we left Maidencombe by a public road going north from the car park then turned left behind the last house. From now on the path has many ups and downs until it meets the A379. In a short distance we left this road and entered the top field above Shaldon, past the pitch and putt course following the path which leads to the top of 'The Ness', a tree covered headland. We now descend to Shaldon walking inland to cross the Teign by the road bridge beyond the shingle bank called 'The Salty', a firm expanse where fishermen dig for bait between the tides. It is of course possible to catch a bus to Dawlish Warren but we choose to walk from Teignmouth through Holcombe to Dawlish, the whole way being mainly built up therefore not nearly so enjoyable as the wild uninhabited coastline we had grown to love. From Teignmouth Pier one soon reaches the limestone sea wall which protects the railway from the waves. Incidentally this railway is the main line between Paddington and Penzance, one of Isambard Kingdom Brunel's great civil engineering achievements. The distance from the ferry to the end of the sea wall is two miles and as we walked along within a few yards of the frequent inter city 125's, memories flooded back to me of the only time I had travelled on this line. It was way back in 1942 as a trainee pilot in the RAF on my way with 42 squadron to take up a new posting in the west country. Almost 50 years ago, now here I was walking it! At the end of the wall you leave behind the sound of the sea before passing through a tunnel beneath the railway to climb up Smugglers Lane joining the A379 for a while until turning into Derncleugh Gardens. After a while the path drops steeply almost to the railway again then climbs up the other side of the valley until a signpost directs the walker inland to follow a winding path to a flight of steps and a stile passing some old farm buildings. Once over the top of the hill we hugged the cliff edge closely, passed two look out posts then down a zigzag path to Dawlish. Heading east, once again walking on the sea wall it is one and three quarter miles to Dawlish Warren. A popular resort for caravan and camping holidays with a designated Eurobeach, chalets, shops, a go-cart track and an amusement arcade which makes this end of Dawlish Warren a lively place during the holiday season, but I must add "not our cup of tea." We continued walking right to the end of the Warren itself. The sand bar across the mouth of the Exe is a 500 acre nature reserve and vast numbers of birds can be seen, in fact flocks of thousands at a time are not unusual, a much more peaceful atmosphere than the fun fair.

24th September 1990
Torquay New Harbour to Maidencombe – 7 miles

A lovely autumn day, even at 7 am it was very warm, and the sun was to shine from dawn to dusk. A day to travel light, not only in clothing, but also in a light-headed mood.

Drove the car to Maidencombe and caught the bus back to Torquay New Harbour. It was from the pier that we set off up Beacon Hill, passing close to the five star Imperial Hotel where one gets a good view of a limestone rock arch with the name of London Bridge. Now some steps lead to Rock End Gardens and in due course onto Daddyhole Plain through another archway at the south corner. This area is considerably built up and for a while we walked along Marine Drive until swinging off to the right to Thatcher Point and eventually through shaded woods to the look out point on Hope's Nose. Moving on, way above Hope Cove next comes the Black Head and once around this obstacle you are high above Anstey's Cove and Redgate Beach with Long Quarry Point's jagged outline appearing to block any further forward progress. All the cliffs are red from Oddicombe Beach onwards except at Petit Tor Point where a huge hole has been quarried out of the cliffs and is known as the Giant's Armchair. With such beautiful weather we decided to dally a while taking a steep woodland trail to reach the most "secret" beach in the Tor Bay area. This shingle cove, favoured by naturalists and sea anglers, lies below cliffs of red creeper covered sandstone, an idyllic spot which holds many happy memories for me. It was in 1946 that my first wife and I honeymooned at Babbacombe and we spent many pleasant hours soaking up the sun in this quiet corner of the coastline.

Back on the high cliffs once more the path continues northwards skirting Torquay's Golf course then dips through Sycamore woods so dense is the leafy canopy that in summer the forest floor gets little sunlight. This is a favoured badger haunt and the wide path is criss-crossed by badger trails giving evidence of many years of occupation. Whilst Maidencombe is but a couple of miles ahead nature throws up more obstacles to the walker in the form of steep cliffs and the aptly named Valley of the Rocks. There is another daunting bit where a ledge has been hacked out of the cliffs, although railings give some sense of security, but anyone lacking a head for heights may have problems here. This section is known as the Goat Path.

Today has given me a great sense of achievement, I had reached Torquay on foot from far off Poole and to celebrate I surprised Ruth by announcing that if a room was available we would abandon our flimsy canvass abode and dine in style, sleeping overnight at the Grand Hotel. The reason behind this proposal was that way back in 1942, The Grand requisitioned by the RAF was in the front line against Hitler's massed troops and the Luftwaffe. I had been stationed in this fine building for many months and although I carefully explained to the rather haughty hotel manager that I had been a long stay guest in the past the fact my previous sojourn had been almost 50 years ago cut no ice with him and I did not get the preferential treatment that I had expected!! 'No, I'm sorry Sir, I haven't a room available with a sea view, but there is one on the third floor that overlooks the railway station at the back.' He replied. Beggars cannot be choosers I suppose. We took it for one night only, but what luxury compared to our little blue tent.

23rd June 1991
Torquay New Harbour to Brixham – 8 miles

After a gap of nine months part of the time spent on a visit to Australia and New Zealand, Ruth and I returned to the south Devon coast picking up the coastal path once more from Torquay Harbour. This time walking west.

We left home on Sunday morning the 23rd of June, drove non-stop 170 miles to camp at Upton Manor Farm, St Mary's Road,

Upper Brixham. It rained heavily all the way down, not a good omen for long distance walking on muddy footpaths. Although we waited patiently until dusk, the downpour failed to relent and we were forced to pitch our tent in a howling gale, with rain sleeting across the site meadow. Despite the fact that we were sheltered to some extent by an overgrown hedge it became almost an impossible task to get the tent erected. I had to hang onto it whilst Ruth struggled desperately to get the guy ropes fastened down but eventually the task was completed. Creeping inside like two half drowned rats we just prayed that our shelter would still be with us next morning. It was, but still it rained. What do the local residents say? "Come to sunny Devon where it rains six days out of seven." Very true!

The first five miles of this section around Torbay is of course urbanised and it mostly means walking on footpaths alongside the railway line or public roads side by side with the hustle of holiday traffic. However there are some pleasant parts like Paignton Sands, Goodrington Sands and Elberry Cove. The last named beach is littered with lovely, wave-washed coloured pebbles which when polished make ideal paper weights. We pottered around collecting those of the correct size but soon realised that pretty pebbles make up unnecessary ballast! And most were reluctantly abandoned. Approaching Beer Head a heavy sea mist made visibility poor which was unfortunate because the scenery around St Mary's Bay is really breathtaking. We took the footpath through Beer Head Country Park and regrettably got lost in the dense woods of the Grove but eventually by keeping the sound of the sea on our right arrived at Brixham Harbour. This attractive fishing port with its narrow streets and brightly painted houses which climb the slopes behind the harbour also boast a full sized replica of The Golden Hind. It looks surprisingly small at anchor in the marina, in fact little larger than the pleasure boats moored alongside it, but the fact is that Sir Francis Drake sailed around the world in 1577-80 in just such a tiny vessel taking with him 10 officers and 80 men. According to the records only 56 crew returned. In marked contrast Ruth and I have sailed to New Zealand via the Panama Canal after first crossing the Atlantic then the vast Pacific Ocean a journey of just six weeks but fortunately we were not quite so cramped for space and we flew back to England in a mere 24 hours!

25th June 1991
Brixham to Kingswear – 8.75 miles

This section of the South West Coastal Path is described in the national trail guide as strenuous. We found this to be an under statement. It had rained all night and was still throwing it down at 7 am. Considering myself as something of a weather prophet I confidently forecast a fine day relying on the old adage 'Rain before seven clear by eleven.' Unfortunately what happens frequently in Berkshire doesn't seem to apply in Devon! We moved off and as the day progressed the weather closed in, rain driven by strong winds blew down the combes and on the high cliffs we were in thick swirling cloud so dense we could see but a few yards. Ruth was concerned that we would get lost, it is so easy to miss the path by following a sheep trail in the wrong direction. She voiced her opinion that she couldn't go on much further yet on the other hand agreed that there was no point in remaining where we were. In this long stretch of coastline we saw no other human being and apart from the row of miners cottages at Mansands we saw no other house or farmstead. There are many small coves and bays which the seabirds enjoy all to themselves. Foxglove, honeysuckle, sweetpeas, horse daises and many other species line the cliff path, a path that zigzags back and forth to such an extent that forward progress was very slow. By midday we were thoroughly drenched, rain ran down our necks and gravity directed it to our feet so that as we walked down hill the water in our boots ran to our toes and walking uphill it swished to our heels, we couldn't have been much wetter if we had fallen into the sea! Tina was drenched too, but undeterred by the weather still managed to retrieve two "mixey" rabbits and seemed most put out when I buried them in an old badger sett. One plus on the way was when crossing a hilly field of fodder turnips we collected a plastic bag full of lovely mushrooms. Our next mornings breakfast was secure assuming we made it back to camp! It was a disappointment that the weather and visibility were so poor. On the first six miles from Sharkham Point this coastline is one of the most beautiful stretches along the entire National Trail, much of course owned by the National Trust. After leaving Scabbacombe Head one comes to the best maintained and most clearly marked section of the walk so far. This much improved path from Newfoundland Cove to near Kingswear castle was opened in memory of Lt-Col H. Jones VC. OBE. hero of the Falklands war. He had strong family connections in this area. At the western end of this splendid length of path we had the experience of climbing the ingenious timber steps built by Alan Pope and unveiled by 'H' Jones widow in 1984. They are indeed a fine and lasting memorial. At this point we felt that we were almost at our journeys end for the day, but not so. It is a very long walk following the river Dart's eastern bank through Warren Woods. This magnificent forest with its huge pine trees was badly damaged by the Great Storm of '87 then again by a disastrous fire at a later date, however, wet and exhausted we arrived in Kingswear just in time to catch the 4.30 pm Great Western 'Devon Belle' steam train back to Paignton, then by bus to our camp site.

26th June 1991

Still raining, but by 10am the rain clouds cleared at last and the sun came out in time to dry some of our wet clothes and the tent before we struck camp. The whole day was to be given over to crossing the river Dart and setting up camp again at Mr. Pratt's Manor Farm, Strete. However we did find time during the day to explore Dartmouth and enjoy a picnic lunch on the quayside surveying a colourful selection of yachts, cabin cruisers, ferries and bigger seagoing ships which throng the Dart in summer.

27th June 1991
Dartmouth to Torcross – 8 miles

For once we were enjoying a bright, warm day, nothing lifts one's spirits more than a dose of summer sun. From Dartmouth Harbour we followed the B3205 along the Dart's western bank past 'One Gunpoint' as far as the castle. Having once more reached the cliffs a fine view unfolds across the estuary to the cliffs east of Kingswear and the forested shoreline we had walked two days previous, whilst to the right, way across the gentle sweep of Start Bay we could pick out the lighthouse on Start Point. We had walked the eastern and western banks for some six miles but now we were making progress westwards once more. The path dips to sea level at Blackstone Point crossing a gully by a wooden footbridge then passes around the back of Compass Cove. In another mile or so we reached Combe Point and here, just off shore are those dangerous wave washed rocks, 'The Dancing Beggars' responsible for many a shipwreck over the years. At Stoke Fleming the path swings inland and for a while we walked along the A379 until reaching 'Blackpool Sands' a sandy cove of fine golden shingle sheltered by high, pine clad cliffs. This beach is part of a private estate and until I walked the coastal path I must admit I didn't know that the Lancashire Blackpool had a namesake, but that is where all resemblance ends. The two Blackpools are as unlike as chalk and cheese. The one up north with its bright lights, noisy funfairs and everything designed to extract the holidaymakers hard earned cash. A stark contrast from the quiet, peaceful southern Blackpool where ones money is restricted to the purchase of little more than an ice cream or a cup of tea and one makes one's own entertainment with nature's free gift of sand and sea.

As one continues westwards there is no coastal path as such for some way, we had to strike inland following a second class road and what was little more than a farm track around Strete until meeting the A379 once more. This is a busy section of road, especially in summer, which meant trailing in single file husband, wife, dog to face oncoming traffic, and keeping our wits about us until we got to Slapton Sands. For three miles the route runs along the sands with the nature reserve of Slapton Ley on the landward side and being flat and level we soon arrived at Torcross our objective for the day.

28th June 1991
East Prawle to Torcross – 7.75 miles

I rose early, in fact in time to watch the sun rise at daybreak which at this time of year was at 4.15am. We were making such good progress with our coastal walk that frequent camp movements were necessary. After an early breakfast we packed our tent and equipment. I must say I had no regrets leaving Farmer Pratt's poorly equipped and far from perfect camp site. The grass had not been cut for weeks, the toilet/shower was situated in one of the farm buildings way across the meadow and the nearest shop which sold very little, was two miles away in the village. In our short stay we were his only customer. He proudly informed us he had run the site since 1945. The only comment I would make is that in the last half century he had made little progress or improvements! By 9.30am I had settled my account with Mr Pratt and we were away, dashing along the coast road to park our car at Torcross from where I telephoned Dave Stewart, the local taxi cab proprietor. This pleasant, bearded ex-naval man drove us to East Prawle, in fact by following a sunken lane which zigzags down from the village he dropped us off at the car park, from which Prawle Point is reached after a ten minute walk. Immediately east of this headland is an excellent example of a raised beach, a section of the coast where the sea has retreated over the years and for several miles the coast path follows a low level route keeping on the seaward side of many small well cultivated fields. Further on are many little coves, some with interesting names, such as Sharpers Cove, Horsely Cove and Stinking Cove but in the main the shore line is rocky and inaccessible with many dangerous rocks offshore. Reaching Woodcombe Valley the path heads inland dog-legging north until it passes in front of some derelict coastguard cottages, then swinging east once more to Lannacombe Beach, a popular playground in summer. Just before reaching Great Mattiscombe Sand are the interesting landmarks called 'The Pinnacles', stacks of glacial heads on schist bases, standing like lonely sentries guarding the cliffs from the eternal onslaught of the waves. Peartree Point, Start Point and beyond it is a wild, dramatic scene, an area where one feels very close to the elemental forces of nature. Once 'around the corner', we set our sights on reaching Beesands a tiny fishing village consisting of just a single row of quaint cottages and a solitary public house set right on the edge of the coastline. We planned to slake our thirst at the pub but unfortunately it was still four miles ahead and 3 o'clock when we eventually arrived, only to find the bar closed until 6pm! We still had fresh water but that's a poor substitute for a pint of real ale.

To close the day on a note of history. One can't miss seeing the black painted American Shearman Tank residing near the car park at Torcross. In World War 2 in exercises for D-Day, this tank sank off a landing craft in Start Bay. In 1980 it was rescued from the seabed and even after forty years under saltwater the tank still functioned. Over one thousand young Americans lost their lives in those wartime exercises, mainly when the Germans made a surprise dawn raid. An action that was kept quiet by our authorities at the time.

It was 4.45 pm on our arrival at Torcross and having failed to find any refreshments en-route we celebrated with a Devon cream tea, disregarding the fact that at that point in time our tent and equipment was still stacked in the back of the car, and we had no place booked to pitch camp. However, we had no problem. Later that day we set up camp at Slapton tent and caravan site. The best yet.

29th June 1991
East Portlemouth to East Prawle – 8 miles

A warm sunny day was forecast. We drove from the camp site to East Prawle, telephoned for Dave Stewart to collect us from the car park at Prawle Point taking us to East Portlemouth. This taxi trip cost £10.90 but it was the only way for us to tackle this very rural section of the south Devon Coastal Path, there are no local buses and very few roads. However once on the path the walk from East Portlemouth is very beautiful with rocky cliffs and little isolated sandy coves where shags and cormorants congregate on Shag Rock, Pig's Nose and the Ham Stone. This length of the path is a good place to observe the dodder, a parasitic plant with tiny flowers and a mass of red tendrils, which appears to suffocate the gorse, its host plant. Almost every bush being shrouded as if under a fine mesh garden fruit net or gossamer blanket. We stopped for a snack on Gammon Head a distinctive headland which shelters remote Maceley Cove, a small bay that can only be reached by a difficult scramble down the cliff but it is well worth the effort involved. Refreshed from this short break we were on our way once more where the path swings in a half circle round the back of Elender Cove to the view point at Signalhouse Point. On the landward side were large numbers of overgrown and long neglected narrow fields enclosed by huge flat upright stones set on edge. These old boundaries are centuries old and I found it difficult to comprehend the labour involved in their construction. Yet I had no doubt they would outlast our traditional post and wire fences back on Mousefield Farm. After a stiff climb we reached Prawle Point, a look out against invaders since early times and Devon's most southerly headland. From here onwards the path was rock strewn, strenuous and difficult, passing Langerstone Point and Gorah Rocks until returning to our parked car at East Prawle.

Approaching Gammon Head

23rd August 1991
Hope Cove to Salcombe – 11 miles

After a lapse of two months we were back in Devon, this time on the western side of the Kingsbridge Estuary, all set to tackle another segment of the coastal path. We had left our cottage home in Berkshire driving 199.9 miles to pitch our tent at Karrageen Caravan and camping site. Now for those of you who don't know the area, there is Outer Hope, Inner Hope, Hope Barton and Hope Cove. We set off from Hope Cove making for the Salcombe Ferry, full of hope I should add. A distance of 11 miles and although graded strenuous it boasts some of the finest coastal walking in South Devon.

From Hope Cove we proceeded to the very tip of Bolt Tail a headland that has witnessed many shipwrecks before turning east past Redrot Cove, Redrot Ledge and Ramillies. This last named after a naval ship which was wrecked off these dangerous cliffs. There is some marvellous scenery as the path rises to Bolberry Down. More than 400 feet above sea level, this expanse of elastic turf, gorse and bracken is a perfect spot for a picnic with commanding views along the coast. The path continues along the crest of a rocky spine with cliffs on one side and a sheep grazed valley on the other. Further on we stopped for a while at Soar Mill Cove, an isolated sandy beach occupied only by a sprinkling of nude sunbathers. Needless to say we did not join them in the altogether, content to cool off by a simple paddle in the sea. A stiff climb out of the valley keeping close to the cliff edge brought us to The Warren, a high level path which continues for some distance until reaching the rugged headland of Bolt Head, a magnificent look out point with wide views in every direction. From here the path descends to Starehole Bay rises once more then passing round the lookout point and the spiky crags of Sharp Tor to eventually pick up Courtenay Walk, a path cut in the last century by the Courtenay family. A pleasant and easy walk of 2 miles to reach Salcombe a favourite haven for yachtsmen and one of the West Country's finest natural harbours.

25th August 1991
Bigbury-on-Sea to Hope Cove – 6 miles

A hot August sun shimmered across the golden landscape. White cotton wool clouds drifted slowly under the pale blue vault of sky and only the occasional puff of warm air rippled the drooping, heavy heads of ripe barley. With a long walk ahead we breakfast lightly on apple juice and cornflakes before packing a single round of sandwiches, an apple each and plenty of liquid refreshment to see us through the day. A telephone call summoned a taxi taking us from the camp site to Bigbury-on-Sea, a busy little holiday village built on low cliffs overlooking a sandy beach which curls round to the River Avon. Since we were heading east we had to cross this river. Walking up the road past Mount Folly Farm we turned right and followed the coastal path down to the southern tip of Cockleridge the terminal for the passenger ferry to Bantham. Having crossed the river we took a short cut across the sand spit called The Ham, then with a final look back across the estuary to Burgh Island, keeping the golf course on the landward side for company we set course for Hope Cove. It was the height of a dry summer, the streams and brooks lacked water and the path was hard and dry. Ruth, lean, fit, and deeply sun-tanned dressed in a faded pair of shorts and light walking boots could out walk and out climb most women half her age even so I found no difficulty keeping pace. On our best day we had covered fifteen miles of often difficult terrain. In today's conditions it was no surprise that we reached Hope Cove by 2pm, in time to watch the sand castle making competition. This was a bonus as we didn't know this annual event was about to take place. Competitors are allocated a marked out square of Hope Cove's golden sand. The construction of each castle must be completed within the hour and parents are allowed to assist their children if they wish. All the accessories such as white pebbles, coloured sea shells, seaweed, flags etc. had been assembled before the start of the competition. Then on the word go a frenzy of activity commences. Soon pre-arranged plans begin to take shape and one realises that not all the modellers are building traditional sand castles. There appear, sculptured in sand, shapes of aeroplanes, motor cars, railway engines, animals and of course realistic replicas of our most famous castles. One enterprising family even constructed a realistic duplicate of Mount Vesuvius with real smoke and flames erupting from the crater and some red material representing the lava flowing down the mountain side. The judge certainly had a difficult task to select the winners in their various classes.

26th August 1991
Bigbury-on-Sea to Wonwell Beach – 6 miles

Still under canvas at Karrageen Camp-site. Few holiday makers are up and around at 7 am and I must say I don't blame them, most come for a relaxing, restful holiday and only the hyperactive like Ruth and I are mad enough to rise early on vacation and tramp 10 or 12 miles every day instead of soaking up the sun on some pleasant wave washed beach. So it was with some surprise that the only person I chanced to meet in the loo block at that early hour turned out to be my son-in-law's father, Harry Bourne. Neither knew of the other's presence on this particular camp site and the only reason Harry was around so early in the morning was because too much wine the previous evening had played havoc with his stomach and disturbed his sleep! We both decided the odds against such a meeting were astronomical.

Today we had planned a moderate walk of about six miles from Bigbury-on-Sea to Wonwell Beach but it didn't work out like that and it was not for the want of trying. We just couldn't get a lift or a taxi and as for buses they just don't exist on this scantily populated side of the Erne Estuary. There was only one thing for it, we parked our car in Bigbury, set off for Wonwell Beach and walked both ways, a hike of twelve tough miles, especially during the heat of the day, by now it was 6 p.m. and our first thoughts were to indulge in a cup of tea at Beach View Cafe then change into swim gear for a well earned dip off the sandy beach which connects Bigbury to Burgh Island. I was rather concerned about my dog Tina she was panting, very hot and rather distressed. Luckily we found a freshwater stream in which she laid for all of twenty minutes before recovering. Today's walk had almost been too much for all of us.

27th August 1991
Erme mouth to Newton Ferrers – 12.5 miles

We moved camp to Brier Hill Farm. Newton Ferrers, driving inland and crossing the River Erme by the first bridge available. We don't usually walk the path on site moving days but we were behind schedule with our double stint of the previous day. Consequently it was 3 pm before setting off from Erme mouth walking westwards to Newton Ferrers, further down the coast. Early on the path is well marked and passes through a succession of arable fields mostly with barley in the process of being harvested. A little further on I was surprised to see a huge herd of friesian dairy cows strip grazing a field of marrow stem kale, this at a time of year when one expects plenty of lush clover to be available. At this point St Anchorite's Rock beckons. A massive rocky tor which looks most impressive from a distance and at first I got the impression it was a church or a castle ahead. The scenery is wild, rocky and the area sparsely populated with lonely isolated coves never visited except by the occasional passing lobster pot fisherman. From the sheltered valley below Carswell Farm we had to tackle one of the steepest hauls on the whole of the path but once on high ground again we reached Revelstoke Drive. Lord Revelstoke whose home was at Membland had this carriageway cut in the nineteenth century to enable him to show off his estate to visiting guests who must surely have been impressed by this superb road and such beautiful scenery, especially if they were out of big inland cities and possibly getting their very first glimpse of the sea. Three cheers for his Lordship, or rather his hard working men. This firm level roadway makes excellent walking conditions, enabling us to stride out, quickly covering the miles to Noss Mayo and Newton Ferrers, even so it was nine p.m. and almost dark before reaching our destination. We had walked for six hours non-stop and it was with some relief that, still dressed in our hiking gear we stopped to enjoy a beer and a bar meal at 'The Old Ship Inn' off Newton Creek.

28th August 1991
Newton Ferrers to Turnchapel (Plymouth) – 11 miles

This last section of the south Devon coastal path took us to the city of Plymouth, something of a 'landmark' an event of some importance to us, because once beyond the River Tamer we would be walking the Cornish coast-line, but first we had to negotiate the river Yealm (pronounced Yam). The passenger ferry only operates in July and August between 1100hrs to 1300 hrs and from 1430 hrs to 1600 hrs. It turned out to be quite a long walk from our camp site to the ferry and there were no visible signs giving directions to the ferry. I enquired of two local ladies gossiping over their garden gates if we were heading in the right direction. "Yes you be m'dear, but we think it closed down years ago", they answered in unison. Now I don't give in easily so we pressed on ignoring their information. Round the next corner we meet an elderly couple out for a stroll. I asked them the same question. "Wots the date and wots the time?" The old gent asked. "The 28th of August and its now 11.30 am", I replied, glancing at my wrist watch. "You should be in luck then. Go down this 'yer road until you come to the little wooden jetty, if he 'ain't there yell ferry as loud as you can and he'll come o'er from t'other side if he be there." We did just that and sure enough after a few minutes a young man came across rowing his tiny boat and ferried us over to the western bank of the river Yealm for a total sum of £2. Tina had no qualms about taking a boat ride! Once across we set off at a cracking pace, when the weather was good it put a bounce into our stride. This section proved very pleasant as the path cuts through cool densely wooded groves of oak, silver birch and sweet chestnut trees. In the sunlit glades of deep woodland, butterflies danced on flickering wings through the motes of green splashed light and once clear of the woods an excellent view of the boat traffic opens up in this busy waterway which sweeps out into Wembury Bay. We pressed on following the path as it cuts across the shoulder of Season Point. It is a lovely area, a place where one gets the feeling of being close to nature. At the side of the dusty, rock scattered track grass hoppers chirrup, while common blues flickered like specks of thrown confetti and skylarks soared skywards. Skirting Blackstone Rocks we dropped down to Wembury Beach where we make a brief stop at the Old Mill Cafe for a much needed cup of coffee before moving on into the clearly marked Danger Area of HMS Cambridge, the Royal Navy gunnery school at Wembury Point. Red flags warned of gunnery practice, hence the guards diverted us to the higher path which actually passes through the naval camp. The fact that two civilians and a dog should be allowed to wander at will in a closely guarded naval establishment with guns firing on the ranges and scores of sailors going about their various duties, seemed a rather odd situation. However once safely through the camp and clear of the high wire fence we picked up the path once more which now takes a right angle turn northwards and at long last we got our first glimpse of Plymouth Breakwater beyond which squat, grey painted battleships rode at anchor with a skyline view of the historic City in the background. Further on the path drops down sharply to Heybrook Bay, crosses a stream then continues following a very rocky shore line for the next two miles. Skirting a large holiday camp on the seaward side a sharp descent takes the walker almost to sea level to cross a deep ravine by a footbridge, by-passing Bovisand Bay, the Fort and harbour. Although on this day's walk we had had some stiff climbs especially at Staddon Heights and the coast guard look out behind Rum Bay it was compensated by long stretches of easy rambles along low cliffs almost at sea level. Another plus was that there was always much to interest us in the shipping activity taking place in 'The Sound.' It had got quite late in the day when we eventually reached Turnchapel yet still I insisted on walking right to the water's edge to gaze across the Cattewater to Cattedown. It is only a narrow strip of water but the lack of a ferry means a detour inland of several miles by way of Laira Bridge which carries the busy A379 over the River Plym. We had no desire to take a very long pedestrian stroll to reach Plymouth City Centre on that particular day, so a halt was thankfully called.

29th August 1991

Moved camp today: With tent and all equipment packed into our little red Peugeot 205 we crossed the Hamoaze by the car ferry to Torpoint setting up camp again at Whitsand Bay Holiday Park, Millbrook. Compared to some of the sites we had stayed on this was indeed 5 Star. Sheltered, yet with marvellous views of the Whitsand Bay it also boasted a large sports ground, heated outdoor swimming pool, showers, sauna, well stocked shop and a smart cafe. Even our little tent cost £9 per night to pitch, a sum I didn't regret paying, for one thing we had at long last reached Cornwall and were about to tackle the Cornish long distance path, a coast line Ruth and I had scant knowledge of, and had seldom visited.

30th August 1991
Cremyll to Portwrinkle – 15 miles

Weather still holding, sunny, good visibility, but rather windy. Away to an early start. We had need for this fine weather as this was to be another maximum stint. Drove our car to Portwrinkle and caught a double decker bus back to Cremyll. We started walking at 10 am and once again the scenery turned out to be different yet we never seemed to tire of a constant diet of sun, sand and sea. Almost immediately after leaving the bus station we entered Mount Edgcumbe Country Park via The Orangery. It is fortunate that this large area, so close to Plymouth is now open to the public. We dawdled in the beautiful grade one listed garden of Mount Edgcumbe House, a Tudor mansion that was rebuilt after being destroyed by bombs in 1941. Leaving the grounds by the far gate the path descends to the amphitheatre where a temple (now in a poor state of repair) overlooks a lake, surrounded by well kept lawns. The walk here is leisurely following the Earl's Drive as it cuts through woodlands of sycamore and evergreen holm oaks, the drive itself shaded by clumps of rhododendrons. Looking out

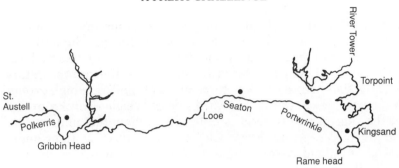

across The Sound one gets a good view from this point of Drake's Island which actually looks closer than it is. Beyond a small beach the path drops down through more open woodland then passing through a double gate one enters a deer enclosure, although we were not lucky enough to see any of these shy animals. It is a beautiful place, quiet and peaceful where one is transported backwards in time and one gets the feeling that it would cause no great surprise if the Earl's horse drawn carriage appeared around the next corner of this cobbled roadway. Having reluctantly left the park we continued to follow the path around Cawsand Bay to Kingsand and Cawsand fascinating twin villages with old colour-washed houses and streets so narrow I was pleased not to be encumbered with a motor vehicle. We had made good progress on the morning walk so did not regret the time spent at the "Rising Sun", a quaint Cornish pub tucked away behind the higgledy-piggledy back alleys of this ancient smuggler's haunt. As an added pleasure we joined a couple of local characters in a pint of the best and a lobster sandwich, to which they extolled colourful tales of smuggling, beach combing and wrecking in days gone by. As they warmed to the subject nothing was lost in the telling and each tried to surpass the other. I suppose I have always been a good listener! On the way once more we turned inland by way of Pier Lane and in due course surmounted a stile, crossed a field of uncut meadow grass reaching on the far side a very old five-bar gate, half open and sagging on rusty hinges, passing through to where the path meets up with the top road near the car park. Our next objective was the Grotto and Penlee Point a view point that allows the walker a last look back towards Plymouth Hoe and the Barbican. One and a half miles ahead stood the lofty summit of Rame Head with its ruined chapel, built at the end of the fourteenth century. We now had before us some three miles of moderate high ground as the path passes to the landward side of Wiggle Cliff. From now on the coastal path walker is obliged to follow the military road for four miles. At Tregantle Cliff the road turns at right angles taking an inland route around Tregantle Fort which at the time was still occupied by the Ministry of Defence and is closed as a danger area with active firing ranges. Safely around this obstacle we left the road for Trethill Cliffs to pass the golf course on the seaward side. There is no path here as such, one walks on the edge of the links following the occasional signpost. Portwrinkle with its tiny harbour is tucked away in a rocky cove, and from the path it comes into view rather unexpectedly, yet were we pleased to see it! I must admit that Ruth and I were just about "shattered" as we dragged reluctant legs the last few hundred yards. The time was 7.15 pm. We had covered 15 miles of often very strenuous walking. A record distance in our book.

31st August 1991
East Looe to Portwrinkle – 8 miles

It was a hot, muggy day in summer with nare a breath of wind, something unusual for Cornwall. Even the birds seemed too tired to sing.

Looe to Portwrinkle. A section with many difficulties, so the guide book states, and in my opinion that is very much an understatement. One of the many obstacles being the Battern Cliffs east of Downderry, also the path in this area is not always clearly defined, and my compass was put to good use.

East and West Looe are linked by an ancient, multi-arched bridge spanning the river, a river born of many tributaries that flow seaward from deep, wooded valleys. A sandy beach at the mouth of the river is sheltered by a jetty known as Banjo Pier named such because of its shape. East Looe with its web of narrow streets and the eastern quay where fishing boats land their catch is an interesting little town and since we were in no great hurry we wandered around for about an hour getting the feel of the place before setting off on our stint for the day. Leaving the old part of Looe we walked up Castle street to an open grass area at the top of the cliffs passing behind the well kept gardens of retirement and holiday homes until dropping down to Millendreath Beach where we stopped for a sandwich and a sip of weak lemon drink from our meagre supplies. Departing from the rock flanked beach by way of an old Cornish lane we turned right at the top to emerge onto Bodigga Cliff, then across a rough, ragwort infested meadow before entering scrubby woods through which the path undulates for some distance. On our transit through the dense undergrowth there was no need to consult the ordnance survey map to pinpoint our position, we had disturbed some rather unusual wildlife. Exotic shrieks and screams on our left-hand side was coming from the Murrayton Monkey Sanctuary. This noisy chatter gave us the impression that we were deep in some South American rain forest instead of on the peaceful south west coast path! Following what was no more than a faint track along the cliff top we eventually descended a long flight of steps to Seaton Beach, a beach of grey sand, pebbles and a large caravan site. Continuing eastwards making for Downderry we were faced with a choice, either to walk the B3247 or walk the concrete sea wall and then the beach. Since the path had petered out and the tide was out we chose the shoreline route. I don't like competing with rushing holiday makers and their assortment of motorised vehicles as they scramble to the coast in search of a parking spot and the last square yard of sand on their favourite beach.

Downderry village, perched on the cliff is squeezed into a long narrow strip of ground between steep slopes and the sea. With houses lining the one and only street it also offers refreshments and accommodation, with shops, parking and The Ship Inn, a pleasant pub with good beer and afternoon cream teas in the cliff top garden overlooking the sand and shingle beach. We made full use of the landlord's hospitality, after all we were only half way on the section we had set ourselves for the day's walk and not only that but the cliffs we had to scale ahead rise to 508 feet beyond Seaton Beach. The path is steep in places, zigzags this way and that until after crossing a field we reached a stile but were unable to see any distinct pathway so we followed the lower edge of another field. From here on to Portwrinkle the path is undefined, we could find no track, no acorn signs we simply kept walking in an easterly direction until taking a right angle turn down a steep narrow lane to emerge in Portwrinkle's tiny harbour. Not only was this the end of a very long, but interesting section of the coastal path but also unfortunately the end of our walking for this year. We had to return to Berkshire, jobs were piling up on the farm.

20th March 1992
Polperro to West Looe – 5 miles

This walking bug seems to be getting hold of Ruth and me. With a few days clear of commitments we were off to an early start for the 1992 season. We chickened out on sleeping rough in our canvass abode, booking in at Little Treque Farm, Polperro. £20 per night in a self catering converted horse stable. Tastefully furnished with colour TV and everything one requires for a 'restful' holiday. The weather, if anything was on the mild side for the time of year, whilst all-round us was evidence of fresh growth and greenery. Unfortunately a dense sea-mist swirled inland making visibility very poor as we commenced walking the coastal path east from Polperro Inner Harbour making for West Looe. Polperro is a picturesque fishing village. Old, whitewashed cottages, crammed together like sardines in a can with astonishing narrow streets from which non-resident traffic is banned but it only took us ten minutes to reach the harbour on foot from the car park. Our walk followed a well marked cliff path through the Warren and on to Talland Bay passing en-route two black and white striped beacons or landmarks. These delineate a nautical measured mile for speed trials off shore. West Looe Down is open pasture land sloping from 300 feet down to the sea. With a strong wind blowing off land it was a bit daunting traversing this steep slope. For one thing the path, if one can call it that is barely 12 inches wide and if you did stumble and started to roll there is nothing to stop you crashing into the hungry waves far below. Of interest on this part of the coastline is Talland Church. We paid a quick visit and signed the visitors book to record our passing. The most unusual feature of this small church is the fact that the tower is built completely separate from the main structure. I could not fathom any logical reason for this architectural anomaly but no doubt it must be recorded in the history of the church. The coast path now hugs the coastline for some miles giving the rambler an excellent view of St George's or Looe Island one of the few inhabited islands off the Cornish coast (apart from the Isles of Scilly). By now we had reached Hannafore, which is the first built up part of West Looe, yet we still had well over a mile to walk before reaching the bridge over the river from where we had terminated our walk the previous Autumn.

21st March 1992
Polruan to Polperro – 7 miles

9:30 am we drove into Polperro and after parking the car in Crumplehorn Car Park took a taxi to Polruan. The charge was £8 plus £2 tip. (I must have been in one of my more generous moods!)

This section of path is perhaps the toughest stretch of walking on the south Cornwall coast and I would warn anyone unused to coastal path walking that they may find it extremely stressful, but having said that one is well rewarded for the effort extended by magnificent sea views. Luckily on this day we had the wind behind us, which was quite a blessing considering that in places the path runs within two or three feet of the cliff edge and at times severe gusts threaten to blow us onto the rocks 250 feet below.

We set off from Polruan walking down a narrow lane to the coastal fields, soon to enter National Trust land. It wasn't long before the coastal path starts a long climb to Blackbottle Rock. At the highest point a seat is conveniently placed and from here one can look across Lantic Bay to the next great obstacle to the walker, namely Pencarrow Head. Despite the strong wind the weather was quite mild and it was noticeable how much more forward spring growth was on the coast compared to back home in Berkshire. Violets, primroses, and other wild flowers lined the path creating a natural garden. At this point there was a choice of two paths, the high or low. We chose to keep on the high cliffs, after all if you drop down to sea level at some stage you have to climb back up again. Shortly the path took a 90 degree turn to the south climbing steadily upwards until reaching Pencarrow Head where we made a brief refreshment stop. Most of our walk today was on National Trust land. I always find that the trustees keep the path in excellent order, also stiles are usually first class and incorporate a doggie stile, a simple lifting device which enables easy passage for elderly and often muddy dogs through the barrier without the chore of having to lift them over. It didn't take my dog Tina long to get the hang of things, waiting expectantly for the oak stake to be lifted.

We continued walking high on the rugged cliffs east of Pencarrow Head for some miles until the path dropped steeply to Lansallos Cove, an unspoilt, peaceful inlet which can be reached in a fifteen minute walk from Lansallos village, an isolated hamlet with a fascinating 14th century church. Once over the stream the path climbs the slope ahead, passing a tall white painted navigation aid marking the dangerous 'Under Rock', 1 mile off shore where you can also make out a buoy. Shortly after, down we went once more through a bracken covered slope to cross yet another small stream, with a hard climb the other side to the summit of a rugged headland, reached by staggering up 167 well made steps plus 150 down the other side – no lifts provided in rural Cornwall and I did religiously count the steps. Once past this obstacle the way was clear to Polperro, where we wasted no time finding a small cafe near the inner harbour. A sign in a window read "Dogs welcome" which meant we could sit inside in comfort and enjoy a well earned scones, jam and cream tea. Often because of Tina one of us goes inside to buy two plastic cups of tea and a bun each, then we sit outside on the pavement if no seats are available!

22nd March 1992
Par Sands to Fowey – 5 miles

From our self catering home we drove to Bodinnick crossing the estuary to Fowey by the car ferry which runs daily from 8 am to dusk. Fowey (pronounced 'foy') is a most attractive town with a charm all of its own, where ocean going ships load china clay and mingle with scores of small craft in this sheltered, natural harbour. Parking our car at Readymoney we took the 10.55 am bus to Par. Rather a late start to the day. We had waited in the hope that the wind would drop and the squally weather improve but our optimism was quickly dashed. Casting caution aside we set out from Par leaving the long, sandy beach behind us, heading directly into the driving rain and a force eight gale, far from ideal walking conditions. When the weather is in this sort of mood on the exposed Cornish cliffs the wind is quite capable of blowing the ears off a donkey. The path runs along low cliffs fringing Par Sands, narrow in places it continues between the cliffs edge and pasture land until after some two miles drops down to the tiny fishing port of Polkerris. An unspoilt village which boasts a little harbour, a sandy beach, the post office and an ancient, restored pub, The Rashliegh Arms. By now we were cold and wet and I was all for taking shelter. Smoke from the pub's chimney indicated that the interior offered warm comfort in front of a log fire and a tot of whisky would not have come amiss. However I was overruled. Ruth insisted that we pressed on, her argument was that if we dared to stop we would never have the courage to get going again in what had become really atrocious weather. My wife's decision was no doubt the correct one but I passed the hostelry reluctantly. Fowey was a long way ahead and baring our way was the

The sun doesn't always shine! Polkerris Harbour

windswept headland of Gribbin Head. Leaving Polkerris we climbed steeply, following a zigzag track through garlic-smelling sycamore woods before emerging onto fields along the cliff-top, now to face a two mile hike climbing steadily to the summit of the 250 foot Gribbin Head with its 84 foot high Mariner's Mark. The red and white striped beacon built in the days of sail to signpost the eastern tip of St Austell Bay. Luckily, once on the eastern side of the Gribbin we were sheltered to some degree from the southwest gale that had plagued us all morning. Now began a steady descent to Polridmouth Cove where trees, shrubs and low cliffs overlook a sandy beach. In fact there are two coves separated by a low bluff, the second has a lake behind it and we crossed to the wooded slope beyond the dam, but before doing so found shelter behind a large rock and proceeded to make short work of our limited refreshments. There is safe bathing at Polridmouth but even in the height of the season one will find no facilities on this beach. Maybe of interest to readers of best sellers, Menabilly House lies just inland behind this wooded combe. The seat of the Rashliegh family for four hundred years, Daphne du Maurier lived there and this was the setting of her novel 'Rebecca.' The path now continues its switchback course first to scale Lankelly Cliff then the even steeper Southground Cliffs to end with a wide detour around Readymoney Cove passing St Catherine's Castle built by Henry V111 as a fort to defend the harbour. Finally, with much relief we reached downtown Fowey, where in the area of the Town Hall we discovered a small cafe, finding solace in a pot of tea for two and a jam doughnut apiece.

23rd March 1992
Mevagissey to Par Sands – 10 miles

Despite very inclement weather Ruth and I decided to attempt the long and difficult coastal path between Mevagissey and Par Sands via Charlestown. Walking north east into bitter March wind which brought prolonged wintry showers and piercing hail storms.

Parking the car in Par we took a taxi to Mevagissey. The driver was a true Cornishman who knew the area well and when informed that we intended to walk to Par along the coast he expressed some misgivings considering the weather conditions, our age, being encumbered with a dog and the fact that it is a very long tough walk even in good weather, also his opinion was that it would take at least six or seven hours. He seemed reluctant to leave us at the set down point and I got the feeling that he considered us completely mad and if asked would have taken us back to Par quite willingly free of charge.

Mevagissey, what a lovely name for a delectable little town. It has extremely narrow streets, old fisherman's cottages and shops which sell everything from fish and chips to Cornish pasties, soft scoop ice cream to souvenirs, and not a supermarket in sight. The town seethes with visitors during the all too short holiday season.

When we were there in March the place was definitely locals only. We left Mevagissey heading north past the site of a Napoleonic War gun battery, climbing steeply behind the toilets to the north side of the inner harbour and the coast guard station. After a series of ups and downs we arrived at the massed ranks of caravans at Pentewan Beach, mostly deserted at this time of year. Somehow we missed the path in Pentewan, taking a public road out of the village. We were looking for a church marked on the map but being unable to find this land mark we ended up crossing fields and stumbling through a private dung strewn farmyard. I could quite understand the farmer's belligerent attitude towards us, especially as we were trailing a mud-splattered dog. I get just as annoyed when townies trespass amongst my livestock back home, on the lame excuse of missing the footpath or searching for mushrooms. We were quickly given marching orders and directions.

This next stretch of the path proved to be strenuous, a real switchback and very debilitating. It also came on to rain heavily and the wind blew as though demented. I put Tina on a secure leash as she was in grave danger of being blown over a cliff edge at any moment. In our case we were forced to bend almost double in order to make any headway into the teeth of the gale. Finally reaching Black Head we took shelter behind a wall, devoured half our rations and waited for the worst of the weather to pass on. There are two deep combes to negotiate on this next stretch to Porthpean and it was whilst on this section that we met another hiker, the only person we were to meet in our six hours walking except of course the belligerent farmer and locals going about their daily tasks in town. Once past Carrickowel Point it was down hill all the way into Charlestown, a charming little port designed by John Smeaton designer of the Eddison Lighthouse. Well worth a longer visit when time allows, but for us time was limited and we were forced to leave setting out due east up the steep cliff path, then through the first of four kissing gates to the point where the path emerges onto the road opposite the Porth Avallen Hotel. As this pair of bedraggled walkers made their way past the front of this luxurious building we could see smartly dressed guests relaxing in the pavilion enjoying late afternoon tea and I couldn't help thinking some folk have discovered a much more leisurely way of spending their time. By the way, later on I did make a note in my diary that if I should ever take a more restful holiday the Porth Avallen Hotel would take some beating.

The route now ran along the top of the cliffs, with the Carlyon Bay Hotel and Golf Club on our left. Walking on the seaward side of the golf course just above the foreshore we came to Spit Point and beyond the unattractive china clay installations which had dominated the scene for most of this stretch. In fact we were to discover that the path actually passes through the works by way of a narrow tarmac track guarded by an eight foot high wire fence, then disappears under the main London Penzance railway line through a gloomy, graffiti decorated tunnel. By the way, some whit has named this pedestrian right of way "Dog Shit Alley." It is well named, you certainly have to watch where you tread. Turning right as we emerged, the footpath shortly joins the busy A3082 which we had to follow for a mile or so, there was no alternative. Crossing over the railway by the gated level crossing we carried on along the flat, residential road lined with a scattering of shops. This was Par, and I was on the lookout for a certain building. The Welcome Home Inn. What a gladsome sight for weary travellers and what a grand name to call a pub!!

Mevagissey to the Lizard via Dodman Point, Nare Head, the Roseland Peninsular and Falmouth itself. This walk was spread over four days.

There are many obstacles to the walker on this section of the coastal path, not least the practical matter of getting across some half-a-dozen water barriers without the necessity to make wide detours inland. Ferries are infrequent or even non-existent. For instance at the inlet of Gillan Creek there is no ferry but the creek can be waded within one hour of low tide. If you miss the tide as we did you have to walk inland for two miles or more to round the head of the creek. In fact there are some thirteen stretches of water that have to be tackled between Falmouth and crossing the Exe. Obstacles they certainly are, but they provided entertaining interludes to our slow pedestrian progress.

The date for this section of the coastal path was commenced May 19th 1992 and for once the weather was perfect as we left home. We drove down the M4, M5, to Plymouth. Crossing the river by the Tamar Bridge, no toll going west. After an uneventful journey of 240 miles we arrived at our destination. Seaview International Holiday Park, Boswinger. Holders of AA Best in Britain a title held since 1984. This park is set in glorious scenery, midway along the gentle southwest coast of Cornwall. The owners claim it enjoys Briton's warmest climate often two degrees warmer than the north coast. The immediate area is one of gentle seas, beautiful sandy beaches, coves, harbours and sub tropical gardens. The first night in our tiny tent we didn't get much sleep. The wind got up and blew quite strongly at times and unfortunately my sleeping mattress proved to have a slow puncture and went flat during the night. The result of this calamity meant that I had to pump the blessed thing up ever two hours or sleep on the rock hard turf! Such are the joys of the open air life. Maybe these trials and tribulations are easier to cope with if one is half a century younger!

20th May 1992
Hemmick Beach to Mevagissey – 7 miles

After an early breakfast, Ruth, Tina and I set off to join the path just half a mile down a high banked road and across a grassy meadow to Hemmick Beach, acknowledged as one of Cornwall's most beautiful coves, south-west facing, with golden sands, rocky pools, filled with interesting marine life and no commercialisation. One could so easily be excused for cancelling a coastal walk and spend the whole day lazily sunning oneself on the beach.

From Hemmick Beach the path rises steeply initially, levels out, dips again, then climbs once more to the 370 foot summit of Dodman Point. Having reached the top of this striking headland the path pleasantly contours the upper slopes with its massive stone cross and well preserved watch house. It is an interesting area with two Bronze age burrows which lie within an Ironage earthworks constructed on a grand scale. This was our first serious walk since March and Ruth recently recovering from a severe cold, found the going tough and we were forced to make frequent stops for her to recover her breath and gain enough energy to continue. The path descending from Dodman Point is rocky and steep, much care is needed, then after turning sharply inland it follows the clifftop high above Bow or Vault Beach. This long stretch of sand

and shingle is lonely, isolated and difficult to get to, yet it is a lovely section of this wild coastline. The day we walked this secluded track there was no wind, just a slight breeze off the sea. Far below the incoming tide lapped gentle on the shingle and all around us were the wild flowers of spring, bluebells, foxgloves, campions, wild thyme, penny wort, thrift, common and gold sapphire, yellow stonecrop and many others clinging to the rocky outcrops creating a natural garden wonderland.

We reached Gorran Haven around 1pm. following the path down Foxhole lane to the little seafront. Here we sat on a wooden bench and enjoyed an ice-cream cornet, whilst watching some local fishermen repairing their nets in the shelter of a small breakwater. It was soon time to move on, we dare not dawdle too long. The last bus left Mevagissey at 5.30pm this was our only means of getting back to the campsite tonight and we still had a long walk ahead. Round the tiny harbour, now behind the ice-cream shop, past the chapel then the path turned sharp right still climbing. On our left a long row of council houses, then the path cuts through a built up area of pleasant retirement homes with lovely well kept gardens all with splendid views out over the bay. The cliff top path to Chapel Point gives access to Great Perhaver Beach. Above Turbot Point there is a field known as Bodrugan's leap. This is said to be the place where Sir Henry Trenowth of nearby Bodrugan spurred his horse over the cliff, in a spectacular leap to escape his enemies in 1485 where a boat was waiting to take him to France. Finally the path crossed an open field in which a large herd of crossbred single suckle cows and their calves were grazing, then over a stile onto a public road which drops down in about a mile to Portmellon and Mevagissey. In fact we had made good time and had almost two hours to wait for our bus, time enough to enjoy a cream tea in one of the many little restaurants that dot the village square. Back again at base camp we were soon enjoying a dip in the pool, then what more fitting end to the day than to sit outside our tiny canvass abode and partake of a double scotch. In fact Ruth drank more than enough and ended up a bit wobbly on her feet!!

21st May 1992
Portloe to Boswinger – 5.5 miles

Camping is great fun when the weather is right but when the rain sheets down and the wind shrieks in from the Atlantic as though demented and every stitch of ones clothing runs with water it is not difficult to think of better ways to take a holiday. However there are the good days and today was one of them. I woke at 4.30 am in time to see the sun rise, climbing quickly, a great red ball up and over a tree capped hill to the east. By 5 am it was broad daylight another hot sunny day was forecast. The previous evening I had booked Abba Taxis from Falmouth to collect us from the campsite and take us to the pretty little fishing village of Portloe. The charge was £9. If there is no local bus service a taxi is the only way we can walk a new section as age and strength bars us from backpacking over long distances. The rocky harbour, overlooked by the 17th century Lugger Hotel, is almost as narrow as the streets. We took the path eastwards which climbs out of the village by way of steep steps leading to the Old Coastguard look-out. It then keeps very close to the cliff edge climbing all the while, cliffs that drop sheer to the strikingly clear water far below. The effect is magnificent and well worth the energy expended. We now followed the path to high level, crossing the sheltered craggy buttress of Hartriza Point. Shag Rock, just out to sea on our right was almost covered with black cormorants which took off at intervals to join flocks of other sea birds which were feeding on a huge shoal of fish just off shore. The shoal, which covered an area as large as four football pitches was a moving mass of literally millions of fish. Slowly it moved further out to sea whilst all the time the predators kept up a relentless attack scooping fish from the waves to devour immediately or to carry back to their young ashore.

The coastal path descends to the twin villages of East and West Portholland, each standing behind a beach in its own valley. Here we took a break, removed heavy walking boots and two pairs of socks to paddle in the sea. Phew! what a relief the cool, salt water gives to hot, blistered feet, even Tina now enjoys a dip having at

A relaxing break

last overcome her initial fear of the waves. Cooler and refreshed we took our leave of the beach on the eastern side, a gentle climb to the cliff top near a row of cottages, the path then follows an uncomplicated route to a gate leading to a field. Here there was a workman cutting back the overgrown sides of the path. He was so engrossed in his task that he gave but a brief nod as we past. For some reason Ruth who was in the lead decided to take a short cut directly across the cultivated field in which was planted kale, the young seedlings just showing through the tilled earth. We hadn't got far when a loud, agitated voice boomed. "Keep to the footpath blast you." We promptly returned to the field edge, keeping to the official route. After all he had spent much time and effort cutting the overgrown briers and greenery for ramblers such as ourselves. Leaving the kale field through a gate we turned right and followed the lower edge of a grass field to a stile which gives access to a public road by a hairpin bend just west of Porthluney Cove. Porthluney Cove is a clean and healthy stretch of sand with safe bathing and a large free car park. In fact Ruth decided it was one of the best beaches she had ever seen. Behind the beach Caerhays Castle nestles amongst the trees with a large natural lake on the eastern side. Highland cattle, ewes and lambs graze in the park. It is an idyllic spot and all privately owned by the Lord of the manor. From here the path bears south, and there is a hard and lengthy climb before the first rise is surmounted, now just ahead at Greeb Point is the rocky headland, which looks for all the world like a crocodile's snout. The path to this summit is rock strewn, steep and dangerous, one has to tread carefully. Just before reaching this point we met two ladies-mother and daughter-they made a comment about my John Deere hat which I was wearing. Their American accent gave away their homeland and naturally they were interested in how I came to be wearing such headgear in the depth of rural Cornwall. I explained to them that Ruth and I had recently returned from a visit to Chicago and the John Deere works at Moline Illinois. "What a small world." How often that saying crops up! The daughter hailed from East Moline and of course knew the area well. Ever ready to profit by such contacts I gave them our Farm Guest House address and suggested that if ever they or their friends wished to stay in our home area there is no better place that they could get Bed & Breakfast at such reasonable rates!

We continued on our way, up, up then down again making frequent stops to admire the scenery, which is always a good excuse to get our breath back. The path twists and turns first one way then the other, zigzagging all the while. One must remember that these ancient tracks have been used for centuries connecting one fishing village to the next. The locals, travellers, and tradesmen with their pack horses would have used these old routes continuously in the past. The evidence of this is plain to see with many sections well sheltered from the winter gales by high earth banks or rock built, ivy covered walls. Mostly they are not wide enough for wheeled vehicles, being only a yard or so wide, and without constant attention these narrow byways soon become impassable. We had been told that the Cornish path was overgrown and difficult to follow. This information proved incorrect. It is in fact well signposted and excellently maintained and only one long wooded section through the private Bosahan estate on the south side of the Helford River was the path so overgrown that it became difficult to penetrate the clinging briers and undergrowth. Eventually after walking for six hours we reached Hemmick Beach, our starting point of the previous day. Then the long, hard drag back to the campsite at Boswinger and the chance to cool off in the swimming pool.

22nd May 1992
Portscatho to Portloe – 7 miles

Weather still warm and dry, but a fairly stiff breeze offshore nevertheless made nearly perfect walking conditions. We drove the car to Portscatho, parked and made arrangements with a Mr Morse who ran a private taxi service to collect us from a given point in Portloe at 6pm, not the Morse of TV fame I hasten to add. This left us six and a half hours to walk seven tough miles of path between these two typical Cornish fishing villages. Ample time for a prolonged lunch break and an old fashioned paddle in the sea at lovely Carne Beach in Gerrans Bay.

Setting off from the clifftop car park the path drops down through several grass fields then down a little flight of stone steps into a steep, gullied track that finally descends to Porthcurnick Beach. With the tide out we strolled across the sand to pick up the coastal path at the far side. At this point we meet a tall, muscular middle aged Canadian whom we had passed the day before whilst walking in the opposite direction. We passed the time of day and chatted for a while, he explained that he came over to walk the footpaths of Britain every May, something he had been doing since 1984. He had started out that morning at 8am and had been completely alone with the birds, the sea and the coastline. In fact we were the only serious walkers he had meet that day!

On reaching the Pendower Hotel the route turns inland but at low tide Pendower Beach and Carne Beach coalesce forming a stretch of sand a mile long. However, one can descend the cliff at this point. Thoughtfully a strong rope is provided to help walkers negotiate this section more safely. We walked along this rugged, rocky beach, it has long tracts of golden sand for the most part and being reluctant to leave such a peaceful spot we sat on a rock at the Carne end to take a well earned refreshment break. I understand that no sewage is discharged in this area and complying fully with the EEC standards it is a designated Euro Beach. From Carne Beach we walked up the road to the east, and around a hairpin bend until coming to a stile signposted "Portloe three and a half miles." Leaving the road the coast path goes through a succession of small fields and past a rocky crag near Carne Farm. After this first climb the path descends steeply to Paradoe Cove past the sad remains of a fisherman's cottage. We now had to climb out of the valley making for the crags of Nare Head, and what a climb it was! Ruth and I took it very carefully because it is rough and rugged and at times the path is very near a drop of hundreds of feet to the crashing waves below. However it is well worth the effort as it is a fine headland bristling with exposed igneous rock and the views are just magnificent. We continued at a high level and entered a dense cover of gorse covered, rocky land where the path dwindled away to nothing. It is one of the few times that we have lost our way, however, climbing higher we found a farmer's tractor track which crossed private land in which Simmental cattle, ewes and lambs were quietly grazing. Keeping parallel with the coast, with the sea on our right we eventually met up again with the main path. We now followed the waymarks down and around Kiberick Cove past a curiously contoured field which is believed to have slipped in the distant past and is now called, you've guessed it, Slip Field. The coast path now rounds the Blouth and drops down almost to sea level before once more climbing up a bracken covered slope. It is a stiff climb and the path zigzags continuously until finally one reaches the top and stays on high ground around Manare Point before dropping down a spiny ridge called "The Jacka." We then descended a long track, down, down to our goal of the day "Portloe."

23rd May 1992
Roseland Peninsular – 6 miles

From the National Trust car park at Porth farm, halfway between Gerrans and St Anthony, Ruth and I completed the circular walk round the coast and creeks of the beautiful, almost sub-tropical Roseland Peninsular. One could easily be tempted to omit this remote headland south of Portscatho, but its very inaccessibility is one of its charms and I'm very pleased that we walked this section.

Leaving the lower grassy car park behind Towan Cottage the path leads to a footbridge over a small stream which in turn gives access to a two mile creekside path which meanders through mature woodlands, carpeted at this time of year with the typical flora that flourishes on this mild southwest coastline. Turning south the path runs along the side of the Percuil River until reaching Place slipway and through the trees one gets fleeting glimpses of many pleasure boats and sailing craft to-ing and fro-ing. Turning inland we climbed a stile and headed for St Anthony's church which is set back in the trees. We were at this point when striding round the corner comes our Canadian acquaintance of the last two days. Ruth stopped in her tracks and just gasped. "I don't believe it, meeting you again, three days on the trot." It was indeed a remarkable coincidence. This time we felt we were destined to know more about him, so we exchanged names and addresses. His name is Charles Simpson who hails from Tyree Cottage, Lake of Bays, Ontario. Passing behind the church, which at the time was having a new roof installed, we continued up the slope walking on the edge of just about the best wheat crop I have ever seen. Well over 4 tonnes to the acre if I'm any judge. Then across an immense south sloping field in which a large flock of sheep were grazing. From the top a panoramic view opens to the northwest. St Mawes with its distinctive castle is just across the mouth of the Percuil River with Falmouth two miles away across the Carrick Roads.

My small pocket compass told me that we were now moving due south towards St Anthony Head with its rather squat lighthouse erected nearly at the waters edge. It was built in 1835 as much to warn seafarers of the deadly Manacles reef further south as to indicate the entrance to Falmouth Harbour. The coast path now crosses a concrete dam built to form a reservoir but now unused and choked with silt. Below this dam are the small beaches of Great and Little Molunan, a lovely spot for a bathe at low tide but time did not allow us this luxury.

On the high part of Drake's Downs the National Trust has erected a toposcope viewfinder, which lines up places of interest around Zone Point. It is the best place in the area for spotting sea birds so the local tourist guides tell us. The coastal path now closely follows the cliff edge, dips across a valley and passes behind Porthbeor Beach. Once past Porthbeor the path wanders eastwards. Turning north once you are round Killigerran Head, you soon reach Towan Beach on which there is a wreck post, a relic of days when the breeches buoy was used by the coastguard service in ship rescues. This beach is of sand and fine shingle and has the tide retreats interesting pools are left amongst the rocks, pools alive with small fish like creatures and miniature crabs, an ideal spot for children to fish and play. The route then passes the beautiful Froe Creek, whose northern bank is shaded by a beech wood where we noticed two or three heron's nests. In a few more miles we reached Porthscatho. It had been relatively easy walking, beautiful weather and the scenery different again from the previous day. The Roseland Peninsular is a quiet and charming part of Cornwall, add the mild climate, what better place to spend a few relaxing days.

24th May 1992
Falmouth to Helford Passage – 8 miles

Moved base camp today. Weather still dry and warm but rather overcast with poor visibility. The reason for moving on is because the River Fal obstructs the foot travellers path, which we crossed by car using the King Harry Ferry. Then turned south on the A39 changing shortly to the A394, through Mabe Burnthouse to the village of Mawnan Smith. Finally finding a farmhouse B & B near Helford Passage. Next day we got a lift into Falmouth and walked west from Swan Pool Beach. The path continues near the cliff edge, but one is protected from the sheer drop to the waves below by a strong wire fence. On the landward side are expensive looking country houses with well kept gardens, lush green lawns, conservatories and swimming pools. As for the path, it is a mass of colour, rhododendron, azaleas and honeysuckle close in on either side. The path turns, dips and climbs and all the while the waves crash on the seaweed covered rocks below. We continued along the cliff top soon reaching Maenporth, a popular, sheltered, sandy cove in Falmouth Bay. It becomes crowded during the holiday season, but there is a pleasant walk southwards over High Cliff and The Hutches to Rosemullion Head. I insisted on continuing until reaching the point of this headland which offers fine views over Falmouth Bay, Ruth was all for taking a short cut across a field but the extra distance is well worth while. The white lighthouse on St Anthony Head is a prominent landmark and we get as always a feeling of good will when we look back across some wide bay and say to each other. "That's where we were walking the day before yesterday." After lunch break on Rosemullion Head we pressed on round Parson's Beach and Toll Point where the path runs clearly along the north shore of the Helford River Estuary. This is a tranquil wonderland of narrow creeks which probe far inland between mature woodland consisting of holm, english oak and colourful clumps of hydrangea. Because of the many creeks and small coves it makes for a long walk before one finally arrives at The Ferry Boat Inn the culmination of today's efforts on the path.

25th May 1992
Porthallow to Helford Passage – 7 miles

From our B & B base at Trebach Farm it was but a short walk down to the beach at Helford Passage. The tiny boat (passengers only) plies back and forth across the estuary from 9.30 am 'til 5pm in summer only. At 9.30 am we were the first and only passengers for the ten minute crossing to the opposite bank, where we had made arrangements with Doug Morse, our friendly local taxi driver to take us to Porthallow further down the coast. This is a pleasing village and we spent a pleasant hour browsing through the quaint little souvenir shop which stocks many unusual items. The Five Pilchards pub displays interesting pictures of The Manacles wrecks and relics from the four masted 'Bay of Panama' which was hurled against the rocks during a wild storm in 1891. This too is well worth a stop over for a pint and a chat with the local fishermen, I can recommend it!

The path is well defined here and follows the cliff top closely, past the large mass of Nare Head and beyond to Nare Point. There are enjoyable views from Nare Head over the wooded Helford Passage estuary and on a clear day can be seen Dodman Point some sixteen miles away and once again we remind ourselves. "We had walked that distant point too." The path drops down to the south bank of the inlet called Gillan Creek and only at low tide can one cross to the other side by making use of large stepping stones in this tidal river. Unfortunately, once again we missed low tide so had no other choice but to make the long detour inland to round the water by the bridge at Carne, a small, secluded and attractive hamlet at the head of Gillan Harbour. We then returned by a narrow tarmac road on the north shore to St Anthony-in-Meneage. This tiny village clusters round a church said to have been founded in the twelfth century by shipwrecked Normans. The legend maintains that they vowed to build a church dedicated to St Anthony if their lives were spared. Leaving Gillan Harbour the path continues behind the church through the private Bosahan estate. A prominent sign states firmly, 'no dogs.' In fact this sign is repeated many times as one passes through the estate. I kept my dog Tina on a tight lead and luckily no one spotted her on the three or four mile track through thick woods along the south bank of the inlet to Helford. This is a most attractive former smugglers haunt, the cottages with their thatched roofs, whitewashed walls and little gardens bright with flowers, are a real delight. We reached Helford at 4pm giving us time to sit outside the village shop and enjoy an ice cream before making the ten minute walk to the ferry. It had been a long walk but not one of the hardest by any means.

3rd July 1992
Porthallow to Coverack – 5.5 miles

Once again bitten by the walking bug Ruth and I returned to Cornwall. This time accompanied by my cousin Jack Perris and his wife Shirley for a week of serious walking. Shirley and myself share one thing in common, both of us have had major heart surgery in the past, full marks to those dedicated surgeons and nursing staff of The National Health Service for our return to full health. On this trip we didn't intend to sleep under canvass but planned to enjoy the luxury of Cornish B & B's. An amusing incident set the holiday off to a good start. I had booked two double rooms with a Mrs Daw. The Bakery Cottage, Coverack. Over the telephone she had said, "You will not have any trouble finding my house, everyone knows me in the village." We duly arrived, but every enquiry for Bakery Cottage drew a blank. I was unlucky in the fact that every person I asked were strangers to the place or foreigners from England. "Drop me off at the pub Jack, someone there will know I'm sure," I said confidently. Entering the smoke filled bar half a dozen locals were sat in the corner chatting over their pints, another leaned on the bar gossiping to the landlord. Not sure which person to address I stood in the centre of the room and said. "Any of you chaps happen to know Mrs Daw of Bakery Cottage?" They all seemed to speak together. "Sure we know the Daws." Pointing to the lone man at the bar one of them said, "And ay noo's too, he be married to her."

Next day we took a taxi from Coverack to Porthallow travelling through a maze of narrow lanes sunk between high grassy banks which sprawled eastwards, off the road between Helston and Lizard Point. Ruth and I had reached Porthallow in May so it was from this village that we continued walking westwards. Unfortunately setting off from the beach we took the wrong path which eventually petered out in old quarry workings and it became increasingly difficult to force our way through. Not an encouraging start for our walking companions whom we had told that "The Coastal Path is well marked and easy to follow." To make matters worse it came on to rain and in no time we were all very cold and wet, despite being well equipped with waterproofs. In due course we did make contact with the official path once more, much to the relief of all. I pointed out to cousin Jack that despite our supposed navigational skills even Ruth and I sometimes got lost. That, I said is all part of the adventure, like the old saying. "The man who never was lost, never went very far!" Rounding Porthkerris Point the rain came down even heavier, we just couldn't go on heading into such atrocious weather so we sought shelter in a tiny cafe at Porthoustock. We didn't realise at the time that we had stumbled on a "Volnay" a small exclusive restaurant run by Steven Collins and Colin Rye. With only seven tables one dines there by reservation only. We booked in there and then taking the only table

One of many beautiful coastal scenes

left for that evening and on our return later what a memorable meal it turned out to be. Before the meal commenced Steven the chef and part owner sat on a chair back in the centre of the dining room and took his attentive guests through every item on the menu, dwelling on each ingredient and its preparation with fervour. One's hardest task was to make a choice from such a menu, the evening simply flew by and we were astounded when it was realised that it was nearly midnight. Still savouring that unforgettable meal I have jumped ahead of myself. From Porthoustock we had more stiff walking to do around Shark's Fin and Manacle Point, the path hugs the coastline to Dean Quarry where one has to follow the sign-posted route through this operative quarry. Granite, mainly for road making is loaded off shore two hours after low tide and upon speaking to a workman he informed me that the rubber conveyer belt can load 11,000 tons aboard ship in one and a half hours! Just how many lorry loads does that represent I wonder?

Luckily the rain eased off as we past through NT property at Lowland Point and the last two miles to Coverack were relatively easy going.

4th July 1992
Cadgwith to Coverack – 6 miles

Independence day in the United States of America but for four walking enthusiasts it meant just another hike round the stiffish cliff path between Cadgwith and Coverack. Squeezed into a narrow valley with pretty thatched cottages lining the cliffs, Cadgwith is a favourite haunt for summer visitors and in the tiny shingle covered cove lies all the paraphernalia of the local offshore fishermen. Through a stone built archway which leads to a cobbled courtyard, just a few strides back from the beach are the old fish cellars now converted into a rather fascinating restaurant. One of their specialities is hot jam doughnuts with lashings of double Cornish cream and although we were all anxious to commence our walk it was unanimously decided that coffee and doughnuts should get priority. A pleasant 30 minutes later we left the village via the steep path which disappears between white painted cottages, then climbing a steep tree lined slope through an area renowned as England's only wood of dwarf elms. We quickly reached Enys Head and from there the path continues along the edge of a high cliff, turning inland to negotiate a small rocky gorge at the mouth of the Poltesco Valley. Down to Kennack Sands where two beaches join at low tide to make this one of the longest stretches of sand on the eastern side of the Lizard Peninsular. It is a popular place for bucket and spade families and also geologists as there are exposures of four different rock types very close together and although I must admit I'm not very knowledgeable on the subject I do try to grasp the inconceivable length of time taken to create the history of rocks. Climbing out of Kennack by way of the eastern cliff the going is clear until the track from Borgwitha farm meets the path. Keeping straight on along the top of the windswept cliffs, we now entered a field by way of a gate, and from there we could see the path going very steeply down to the stream at the bottom of Downas Valley, and unfortunately just as steeply up the other side!! At the top of this climb we came to Beagles Point, Pedn Boar and shortly afterwards, Black Head. Lonely, isolated and dramatic these rocky cliffs, rising sheer from the sea. Home to multitudes of seabirds one of which is the Kittiwake, distinguished by their cry-hence the name-and black wing tips. These gulls live at sea for most of their lives but return to these cliffs to breed. Bird life is a constant source of interest as you walk along the path. Some experience of bird identification is advantageous but even with my limited knowledge by making use of binoculars and a good bird book quite a few rare species were observed particularly on this section.

5th July 1992
Kynance Cove to Cadgwith – 7 miles

Today we 'up't sticks.' In plain English, packed our suitcase, paid the bill and took our leave of Mrs Daw and Bakery Cottage, moving to a delightful, homely B & B run by Mrs Johnston, 'Moorland' Prazegooth Road, Cadgwith. This provided a good base to walk mainland Britain's most southerly point.

Next morning after enjoying a first rate rasher and egg breakfast – something I wouldn't indulge in back home – Mr Robert Johnston kindly offered to drive us to Kynance Cove from where we had planned to walk the seven miles back around the coast to Cadgwith in what turned out to be perfect walking conditions. Dry, sunny with a gentle breeze from the northeast.

Kynance Cove. Cliffs two hundred feet high rise on either side of this truly spectacular cove whose sandy beach is completely covered at high tide. Of futher interest is the fact that because of a mixture of hard and soft rocks this has enabled the sea to carve the cliffs into caves, arches and tidal inlets. The most dramatic feature is a fissure through which the sea roars and spurts like a huge steam engine.

There are a multitude of well walked paths criss-crossing the Lizard Downs in this area but the main path crosses a footbridge over a stream then continues up steps to the top of the cliffs past the car park and cafe at the Point. Here, I must admit we didn't pass the cafe, at least not until we had sat outside on a hard wooden bench to partake of a cup of coffee and a sticky bun! Having rounded the corner, so to speak, the path continues high above rock wave-washed cliffs. On the seaward side beyond Polbream Cove and Bumble Rock is the Lion's Den, a hole in the cliffs formed one stormy night in 1847 when a cave roof collapsed, but from above it didn't look that spectacular. What I did find more interesting as we walked round 'Housel Cove' was the fact that it was from the high cliff of Pen Olver that the Spanish Armada was first sighted in 1588. This must have been quite a sight and caused much consternation amongst the local population. Another point of interest is the signal station, a building from where Marconi conducted his radio experiments, making contact with the Isle of Wight in 1901. What a surprise this inventive gentleman would have if he came back to witness the vast strides made in telecommunications today.

Rounding Bass Point and secondly Hot Point – it was certainly hot here too – sheltered from the wind the sun blazed down. Cousin Jack's bare head soon acquired a suntan and was hot enough to fry an egg on he maintained proudly. We next reached the lifeboat station at Church Cove. It is only when one reads the long list of shipwrecks these brave volunteers have attended over the years that you can appreciate the risk they frequently take in the Atlantic's worst storms. In a few more miles we reached Cadgwith but not before gazing with some awe to the depth of The Devils Frying Pan. A 200 foot deep hole caused by the collapse of a huge cave in the distant past. Finally over the last stile, up the last steep slope, round the last corner four pairs of ageing legs were giving vent to overuse.

6th July 1992
Kynance Cove to Poldhu Cove – 6 miles

Today we moved base camp once again, this time to stay with Barbara and John Rosindale at Treworder Farm. A converted barn in a courtyard setting watched over by the ivy clad church tower. It is quiet and secluded but only 75 yards from the village centre of Ruan Minor. Once again the generosity of our host solved our transport problems when John Rosindale kindly offered to act as unpaid chauffeur. The walk on the western side of the Lizard Peninsular from Kynance Cove to Poldhu Cove is once again a tough one, for instance one has to tackle Predannack Head, which rises some 260 feet above the sea but is well worth the effort for the wonderful view embracing the whole of Mount's Bay. Leaving the cove in a mainly northern direction there is a steep climb to the top of Kynance Cliff, from where one gets a marvellous view of the four main islands just a short distance offshore. Asparagus Island, Sugar Loaf Rock, The Bellows and The Bishop, formed of serpentine rock, they rise sheer from the sands and can be reached on foot within two and a half hours of low tide. The path continues past Rill Point, (it is claimed that the Spanish Armada was first sighted here, a more likely spot than round the corner on the far side of the Lizard in my opinion), then across open moorland with only the solitary Kynance Farm in view. Apparently the land in this area is very infertile, waterlogged and almost impossible to walk across in winter. Now given over to a nature reserve, plants grow here in perfusion as no where else in Britain. Cornish heath with its pink and white flowers for instance thrive in this peculiar serpentine soil and a general lack of agricultural activity goes a long way towards creating an unspoilt natural environment. Unfortunately the quiet and peaceful walk through this almost uninhabited side of the Lizard Peninsular which we had been looking forward to was completely shattered by the continuous activity of naval helicopters flying very low overhead from the Predannack Airfield on what was obviously some air sea rescue practice. At this point the path is very close to the edge of precipitous cliffs around Vellan Head, Pol Cornick and

Predannack Head. Unfortunately we were walking into a stiff head-wind which caused Shirley some distress with the result that she and Ruth gave up at Mullion Cove. Jack and I continued on around Polurrian Cove, where on high ground just beyond the cove is the Marconi Memorial which stands near the spot from where the first radio message was transmitted across the Atlantic on December 1st 1901 being received at St. John's Newfoundland almost 3000 miles away. The progress made in telecommunications in the last 90 years is absolutely staggering. I just wonder what the next 90 years will bring?

Thankfully we dropped down the last bracken covered slope into Poldhu Cove where our respective spouse awaited our safe return.

7th July 1992
Porthleven to Poldhu – 5.5 miles

Shirley, suffering from a touch of the sun and still exhausted by yesterday's effort had declined to join us on today's walk. Jack drove Ruth and me to Porthleven the little town with the big harbour which stands on an attractive section of the coastal path. Unfortunately it was 11am before we got on our way, striding briskly southeast towards Poldhu Cove our destination for the day. To reach the path we followed the cliff road climbing out of the town at the far eastern end of the harbour. Past some old cottages and the coastguard lookout until reaching Loe Bar which was formed by the damming of the River Cober and a bank of shingle being built up by the sea, creating Loe Pool a beautiful freshwater lake more than a mile long and a haven for multitudes of water birds, also incidentally the largest natural body of fresh water in Cornwall. Whilst crossing Loe Bar Ruth and I came across a well constructed maze, built with large stones probably by parent assisted children. I decided to give it a try. Although reasonable easy to reach the centre I found it a devil of a job to get

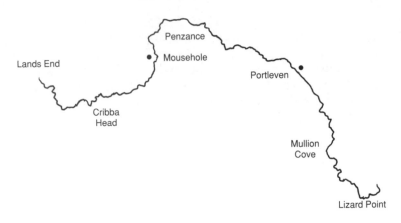

out again, that is without cheating and crossing blocked off sections. Leaving the Bar after this interesting interlude we continued up an easy slope past a white cross sacred to the memory of about a hundred officers and men of H M S Anson who were drowned when their ship was wrecked on Loe Bar in 1807 and buried in this area. Before reaching Gunwalloe Cove we made a bad decision, taking the lower path which traversed a very steep, grassy slope. The path deteriorated until it was no more than 10 inches wide and followed the unprotected cliff often within feet of the edge with a sheer drop to the sand beach below, we had obviously been following a sheep track. Ruth was all for turning back, but I figured that as we were more than halfway across, I felt it wise to press on. We breathed a sigh of relief when Gunwalloe's long gravelly beach lay just ahead. At this point we stopped for our lunch break, sheltering in the shade of an old ruin. Refreshed we moved on, leaving Gunwalloe behind, the path wanders up to the 200 foot contour line and then alongside the main road around earth and stone banked fields of Halzephron Cliff. From this high point the path descends to Church Cove, a crowded beach in summer. Ruth and I spent a quiet hour inside the little church of St Wynwalloe. It is 15th century and for some reason has its belfry, which is 200 years older, separate from the church and half buried in the sandhills. No doubt because the sand

80

dunes have moved inland over the centuries. In the visitors book for the date of 7/7/1992 will be found our name and address. If any of my readers should visit this part of Cornwall this interesting church is well worth a visit. Following the steep path along the golf course we arrived at Poldhu, journeys end for the day.

8th July 1992
Porthleven to Bessy's Cove – 6 miles

The last section of coastal path we walked on this trip to Cornwall.

Before setting off from Porthleven we enjoyed a cup of coffee in a small cafe by the harbour wall. Arrangements had been made for Jack and Shirley to meet us at Prussia Cove at 4 pm. Since the walk was described as moderate we would be under no great pressure to make the six miles or so on time. Leaving Porthleven by way of Mount Pleasant road we soon left houses, roads and civilisation behind. The path scenery was different again in this area, for instance on both sides of the track grew great banks of yarrow. Farmers and gardeners may call it a weed but in this setting it looked quite colourful with it's dull white and pinkish flower heads in close flat clusters. Apparently it is really a herb, common on roadsides, dry meadows and waste ground also I couldn't but fail to admire the lovely old rock covered soil walls which protect the path and divide the tiny cliff-side fields in this part of Cornwall. These walls, built on the seaward side were there really to protect and shelter the coast guards who patrolled on foot these cliffs in times past, and thankfully I gave a silent prayer for those long dead workmen who had created them.

The line of the path is clear and has been diverted back from the dangerous cliff edges which are always giving way, yet not too far back for the discerning ornithologist to get a good view of fulmers and herring gulls on their nesting sites. Round the next promontory we continued halfway down the cliff, here on a wild section of the coast are the ruins of the engine house of the Wheal

Trewavas perched on the steep granite face of Trewavas Head. Copper ore was mined from under the sea until 1850 when water broke in and the whole project was shut down. Half a mile further west at Rinsey Head one passes the engine house and chimney of Wheal Prosper, another old copper mine now partly restored by The National Trust, which stands these days as a memorial to Cornwall's mining days in the 18th and 19th. centuries. An interesting point here: The locals do say that since so much mining was carried out in Cornwall in days gone by, that there is as much air underground as there is on top!

Praa Sands, a sandy strip 1 mile long, with a banking of high dunes. Ruth and I marched confidently along keeping close to the sea where the washed sand is much firmer. What a relief to be able to walk in a straight line on level ground. If all the coastal path was like this we would be at Lands End by tomorrow evening, after all we can see our goal at last, just twenty miles away across Mounts Bay. Well, perhaps we are being optimistic, it is probably Gwennap Head, but Land's End is only a mile or two round the corner!

Constantly, whilst walking the coastal path we remind ourselves that around ever bend and every headland the view is different again, a new vista, a new panorama emerges. It is magic and often holds one spellbound. The sound of the waves on the rocks, the smell of the sea, the screeching gulls in a clear blue sky, and the sight of huge waves breaking onto a desolate beach. Contented sheep and cows lie in the shelter of solid granite walls. Granite is everywhere in this part of Cornwall, in the construction of houses, barns and outbuildings, even the Celtic crosses and the Merry Maidens stone circle still stand solid and unmoved after thousands of years. The holiday maker who dashes down to England's most western point spends a few hours there and thinks he has seen it all is under a misconception. The best way to see Lands End and the surrounding countryside is to don a stout pair of boots and walk there!

3rd August 1992
Bessy's Cove to Penzance – 7 miles

On the 3rd of August 1992 Ruth, myself and grandson Edward set off from Bessy's Cove, the spot where we had left off walking the previous month. Negotiating the rocky headland of Cudden Point one soon reaches Prussian Cove. This jagged cleft in the coast is a narrow opening leading back right into the cliffs enclosing a small, sheltered, sandy beach. Quite an attraction for the few people who make the effort to reach this secluded spot. Pressing on we stayed on the clifftop above Praa Sands until reaching Maen-du Point here we were forced to descend to the beach which was just a jumble of giant pebbles many of which were three, four or even five times as large as footballs. With the sea on one side and an unclimbable cliff on the other there was just no way round this latest obstacle and for quite a few hundred yards we scrambled gingerly over wet seaweed encrusted stones. Our dog Tina, usually sure footed, found the going extremely difficult and not at all to her liking. Back once more on the cliff top the path runs alongside numerous small fields of quite fertile soil. Early potatoes followed by broccoli (a hardy variety of cauliflower) seems to be the main crop, although we did notice that daffodil bulbs were an alternative. Upon reaching Marazion we walked down Turnpike Hill into the centre of this small attractive town which lays claim to being the gateway to St Michael's Mount. With the tide well out we walked the causeway over to this granite island which rises 300 feet from the waters of Mount's Bay and looks from a distance like some giant's sand castle. This days walk, apart from the giant pebbles had been relatively easy, so to celebrate, much to Edward's delight we broke the rules and bought an ice-cream each. Finally we decided to call it a day just short of Penzance. With the main road and the railway running alongside the beach it is an unattractive part of the coast path.

4th August 1992
Lamorna Cove, Newlyn and Penzance via Mousefield-whoops I mean Mousehole(pronounced mowzul) – 4 miles

A stiff climb out of Lamorna Cove brought us to the headland, Carn-du. The steep bracken clad slopes above the bay are studded with huge blocks from the quarries, last worked in the 19th century and subsequently shipped out from Lamorna's tiny harbour. The path then deviates inland through Kemyel Crease Nature reserve, a dark wooded section with a dense cover of pine, oak and chestnut trees. Blue and white hydrangea give colour to the route until one suddenly emerges onto a grassy plateau with a good view of St Michael's Mount across the Bay. We continued climbing to reach the coast guard lookout, and then one must walk along a tarmac road into Mousehole, once Cornwall's main fishing port. With its narrow streets, interesting shops and stone built cottages which close in on the village snug little harbour it is well worth a visit. We just sat on a bench thankful for the rest and watched the world go by until moving on again into Newlyn and Penzance.

5th August 1992
Porthcurno to Lamorna Cove – 5 miles

High on the granite cliffs which shelter Porthcurno from the western gales is the remarkable and romantic Minack Theatre where plays are staged in the open air. A performance in this magnificent setting is a great experience but be warned the rock seats can be hard, so do take a cushion and it can get awfully chilly when the sun goes down! Very steep steps lead down, down, down to Porthcurno's beach of minute white shells and Rowena Cade's tiny beach house. In fact there is a sign at the top of the steps warning children and elderly persons not to attempt this descent, it did cross my mind that at 71 years of age should one consider ones-self elderly? Leaving the cove we climbed to the cliff-top

'Which Way now Grandad?' asks a bemused Edward

opposite, stopping briefly at the white pyramid close to the path which is a guide to shipping and also marks the spot that the first transatlantic cable came ashore in 1880. The next landmark is the headland Treryn Dinas an ancient fortress settlement with an iron age cliff castle. Also on this point is Logan Rock, an 80 ton rocking stone, now that is something that should be easy to find or so we thought. We discovered many unusual shaped rocks precariously balanced but couldn't be sure that we had seen this huge boulder which can apparently be made to wobble with nothing more than a hefty push!

We stopped for our lunch break at Penberth Cove, an unspoilt spot, popular with artists and often described as "The most perfect of Cornish fishing coves." It has a small stream, just a few cottages and local fishing boats beached above the rocky shore.

Also of interest was the unusual capstan that resembles a great cartwheel laid on its side, this was once used to haul larger craft up from the sea. On the occasion of our visit holiday makers were non existent and I guess it never becomes crowded with a car park for only about six cars way up the lane. Leaving Penberth it is noticeable how the vegetation changes on this more sheltered coastline. The dry heathland is dominated by bell heather and a variety of mosses and lichens with very few trees or shrubs. There are some strenuous climbs to the cliff top above Porthguarnon and Coffin Rock until the path drops through a small wood to the waters edge at St Loy. We walked along the beach until almost hidden behind a massive boulder the path leaves the shore and zigzags inland and upwards then turns to meet Boscawen Point and Tater-du. From this point on the path keeps to the cliff top and along the whole length of Tregurnow Cliff one walks on the very edge of the cliffs two hundred feet or so above wicked looking wave washed rocks. On reaching Lamorna Cove we made our way inland to the village partaking of a well earned beer at the Lamorna Inn, known locally as "The Wink." Apparently the nickname goes back to the time when spirits were barred, but a wink in the right direction would quickly produce smuggled brandy at a discount!

6th August 1992
Last lap on the south coast: Porthcurno to Land's End – 4.5 miles

Setting out from Porthcurno on a perfect summers day my wife and I were accompanied by my stepdaughter Sue Bourne, her husband Roger and our grandchildren Edward and Catherine. I had doubts whether Ruth and I would be able to keep pace with the young bloods, yet later they confessed that they too had had fears of Ruth and I "The Professionals" as they called us setting too fast a pace for them! They did adjust to our leisurely walking speed in due course, we had found from past experience that with an initial quick pace, one would not last the day.

The cliff top path by-passes St Levan which is a quarter mile inland, a steep scramble leads down to Porth Chapel, a beautiful,

Land's End at last

cliff flanked cove with smooth rocks and a small, sandy beach. We couldn't resist the temptation to drop haversacks, remove heavy hiking boots, two pairs of socks and get our feet in the brine. The beach shelves steeply, with huge rollers and a strong undercurrent, swimmers are well advised not to venture too far out. Our next stop was Porthgwarra an enchanting spot at the end of a grassy valley with just a few scattered cottages, we stayed there only briefly, just time in fact to sit on a rock licking ice-cream cornets. The strict rules broken once again-three cheers for grandchildren! The path from now on provides magnificent cliff walking especially around Gwennap Head. The sheer cliffs in this area are used as a challenge for commandos and other expert climbers who fearlessly tackle these perpendicular rock faces. Routes with such names as Seal Slab, Commando Crawl and Pendulum Chimney. From now on the path to Land's End is well defined over boulder-strewn grass and heather, but one has little shelter in rough weather. We kept to the cliff-top to circle Mill Bay, from now on to Land's End the scenery is some of the finest of the whole coastal path. The Armed Knight a rocky isle is one of the last land marks before we reached our goal, that great mass of wave washed granite which marks the south western tip of Britain's mainland. When Ruth and I set off from Poole I didn't really think we would ever make the 350 mile coastal path walk to Land's End, but finally on 6th August 1992 we made it! Since we only averaged seven or eight miles per day this journey represents some six or seven weeks of foot slogging. Tramping up and down steep headlands rounding innumerable bays and coves, taking circuitous routes to negotiate South Devon's wooded combes, and hard slogs along sandy or shingle beaches in sunshine, sea mists, pouring rain and force 9 gales, but every day was different, around every headland a different view and fellow walkers we met en-route were always friendly and helpful.

Land's End northwards
The north Cornish coast path traces a very tortuous route, with dramatic heights and stunning views into the distance. In several places the path climbs to over 1000 feet above the sea and often

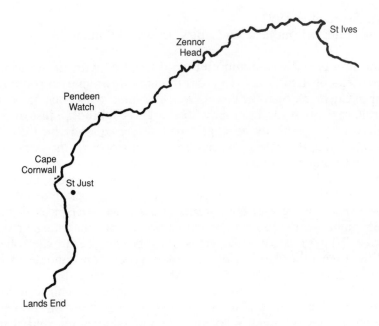

runs along the steep cliff top slopes at around the 700 feet mark. A walk that is not for those of nervous temperament. From Land's End to the Cornish Devon border at Marshland Mouth it is 130.75 miles. Having at long last rounded the corner of England's most westerly mainland point Ruth and I turned northwards with high hopes of reaching Minehead in Somerset by the end of summer 1993, but now it was autumn 1992 and the forthcoming winter would soon see these two enthusiastic walkers on the motorised homeward trail. The thought of log fires and easy chairs acted like a magnet and appeared much more attractive than fighting our way into the teeth of a biting headwind.

30th September 1992
Lands End to Botallack via Cape Cornwall – 9 miles

9am on a beautiful autumn morning found my wife and I turning our backs on Land's End to cross the high downland en route for Cape Cornwall via Sennen Cove. Looking back one gets an excellent view of the Longships Reef and its lighthouse just over a mile offshore, with its helicopter pad sitting squarely on the top. After a while the path plunges down steep slopes to the attractive little harbour of Sennen with its huddle of thatched whitewashed cottages and the pub. As we were there at quite an early hour we had the satisfaction of seeing two fishing boats dock and unload. The fishermen were in high spirits and seemed well pleased with their nights work. From the harbour we set out marching briskly across Whitesand Bay, a superb surfing beach where huge rollers follow each other landwards in endless procession unhindered by any landmass this side of North America. Leaving the beach the path climbs steeply upwards and it is sometimes difficult to follow due to the fact that so many paths diverge, branching off amongst the old mine workings. Dangerous abandoned pit shafts and heaps of rock spoil desecrate what would otherwise be really beautiful scenery in this area. On the hill near Polpry Cove, having covered a fair amount of ground we decide to take a short break amongst tumuli. Granite slabs make grand seats and in this quiet spot, rarely visited by the public we spent some time with our binoculars watching what I thought were quite rare birds possibly blown across from America. Cape Cornwall, despite its grand name is not a particular lofty headland. As one approaches the path zigzags downwards almost to sea level then climbs again until reaching the summit where a tall brick chimney stands like a sentinel on the highest point. Cape Cornwall was once considered England's most westerly point but in fact Land's End wins by a mere 1000 yards, just a short head in racing terms, but unlike crowded, commercialised Land's End where everything from car parking to ice creams, from fun rides to the legendary Lost Labyrinth are at sky high prices Cape Cornwall is quiet, peaceful and unspoilt. Only one little wooden hut offers visitors anything in the way of refreshments.

Cape Cornwall

Continuing northeast we had to make two long detours inland to negotiate deep valleys through which fast streams of water gushed seawards and all the while there is much evidence of past mining activities and disused quarries, though thankfully the old shafts are hidden by dense undergrowth and securely fenced off for safety sake. Upon reaching Kenidjack Castle we turned inland to finish our walk for the day at Botallack. It had taken us seven and a half hours of well nigh non-stop walking.

1st October 1992
Pendeen to Botallack – 3 miles

Dry morning but rain forecast later in the day.

Ruth and I having walked well over 350 miles of the coastal path from distant Poole in Dorset, in the main with only our own company except for my dog Tina, today we took the opportunity to join an organised group of some thirty ramblers. Jim Hosking a Cornish farmer friend of mine explained that just by chance they would be walking the very same section that we had planned for this day. The only disadvantage to us was that it was a circular tour setting off from Pendeen car park, first along a public road then following a footpath across farmland until descending a rugged, fern clad slope to reach the beach at Portheras Cove. From here we turned back south following the coastal path and soon reached Pendeen Watch. Incidentally the lighthouse on the headland was opened in 1900 as previously there had been many wrecks particularly on Gurnard's Head and The Wra, or Three Stone Oar as Jim called it. It was at this point that our group leader suggested an early lunch break as rain looked imminent. It was a sensible decision because sitting on wet grass in a downpour is not ideal conditions for a picnic! Sure enough, just as we were ready to commence walking it started to rain in earnest and as the afternoon past it became increasingly heavier until we were all very wet indeed by the time we eventually reached our destination at Botallack. The company had been great, except for a grumpy

92

lady in the party who informed me in no uncertain terms that walkers with dogs must stay at the back of the line. Time passes very quickly walking with people who obviously enjoy the open air life even if the weather is inclement. The scenery on this section is nothing to shout about simply because it has been spoilt by man's activities in the past. Evidence of mining is found everywhere on this coast. The next two days would see us attempt the walk from Portheras Cove northwards to St Ives. The grading is classified as severe and it is the longest and most deserted stretch of coastline on the whole of the South West Coast Path. For many miles there are no shops, pubs or cafes and only one possible place of refreshment and that is at the 'Weary Traveller' about 200 yards from the path along the road leading to the National Trust's beam engine at the Levant Mine. There is not even a telephone box or any means to call assistance if help is required. I should mention here that Ruth and I were very grateful for the hospitality shown to us by the Landlord of this hostilery and I suspect we will not be the last.

2nd October 1992
Pendeen Watch to Zennor – 6 miles

The weather forecast. A rough day with heavy showers, colder.

Drove our car to Zennor, parked in a tiny car park by a disused chapel. Then Jim who had followed in his car, drove us to Chypraze, a tiny hamlet which consists of just a lonely farm and a house or two hidden away down a dead end track. Our walk for the day commenced on the north side of Portheras Cove and it was to be a six mile tramp back to Zennor to complete this section. Once we had climbed the cliff the walking was moderately easy as the path followed the cliff top, but later the weather deteriorated. In a number of places it was quite boggy although some attempt had been made to solve the problem by using pieces of broken paving stones. The stretch between Greeb Point and Porthmeor Cove was particularly difficult and impossible to walk on the correct route all the way, and all the time you must watch where you placed each step. The next obstacle was the great granite mass of Bosigran Cliff and again care has to be taken because many of the paths end at the top of sheer rock faces. These are more suitable for rock climbers or abseiling and we stopped to watch an ascent through binoculars as we approached, but this sport is not for me! I'm not too keen on perpendicular heights. Also of interest on these windswept cliffs, if you search carefully you will find a flock of Manx Loghtan, a rare bred of primitive sheep. They have been brought in as an experiment to keep the rough grazing under control. They get a living from this rough terrain, where other sheep would starve.

By now the wind had reached gale force and I make good use of my walking stick as a third leg for support. The wind sure can blow on the exposed north Cornish coast, I vouch for that. Locals warn you that if you don't take shelter in a gale it will blow the nails right out of your boots! But we were OK, modern walking boots don't have nails in them. The next landmark on our route was Gurnard's Head which is supposed to bear a similarity to the fish of that name. Looking back south westwards, these rocks did look surprisingly like that rather ugly, cold-blooded, back-boned animal. A little further on past Treen Cove whilst negotiating a remote combe we found the spectacular Royal Fern. Nationally it is rare but occurs fairly common in Cornwall. We also discovered several orchids and bog asphodel which grow in these poorly drained soils. These discoveries are what makes walking the coastal path so interesting. Ruth and I maintain that "Around every headland, cove and cliff there is something different to behold." The unknown certainly spurs one onwards.

At times the wind screeched and blew as though demented and we sought shelter during the heaviest storms and eventually reached Pendour Cove which is also known as Mermaid Cove. The story goes that a certain Matthew Trewhella, a tenor in the choir, followed the mermaid down to the sea at Pendour Cove to a spot beneath the cliffs at Zennor Head. The couple were never seen again, but legend relates that their sweet singing is sometimes heard at night. But Cornwall of course is full of such tales. We

Ruth on top of Golden Cap, Dorset

Sister Delcie and Ruth on the path out of Clovelly

Rockham Bay with the lighthouse on Bull Point

Soar Mill Cove

reached the tiny village of Zennor at 4.30pm. We had been walking for five and a half hours.

3rd October 1992
Zennor to St Ives – 5 miles

The weather was still dull with a fine drizzle blowing off the sea, which made visibility poor.

Jim Hosking kindly drove Ruth and me to Zennor where we arrived by 9.30 am. Before leaving the village we first paid a short visit to St Senara's church. The best known feature in this ancient church is the Mermaid Chair, whose medieval carving depicts a mermaid with a mirror in one hand and a comb in the other. Conveniently situated by the church stands the pub, with seats outside, but it was too early in the day to sample the ale so we set forth for St Ives by the much longer coastal route, taking the path out to Zennor Head where there are remains of an Iron Age cliff castle, ramparts and hut circles. On the landward side in this area are hundreds of tiny medieval fields each enclosed by granite walls. It is hard to imagine the immense amount of manual labour involved in building these boundaries even though there is no shortage of material. Today farmers in these environmentally sensitive areas are invited to take part in a scheme whereby they are paid a grant to farm traditionally which amongst other things means maintaining existing field patterns, grazing rough land with livestock and not using pesticides or fertiliser on it. The going is rough, the path for want of a better name, zigzags back and forth, up and down, at times you have to squeeze between huge granite boulders, some as big as a house, little ones the size of a motor car. It really is a moon like terrain, and impossible to follow a set path but as long as we could keep roughly parallel with the sea it didn't matter too much. Seals appear to be fairly plentiful off this wild coastline, so much so that when seen swimming in the rough sea below or basking on a rock we barely gave them a second glance. We did in fact see far more seals than people on this section of our walk. After rounding Clodgy Point we were soon marching across the gritty sands of Porthmeor Beach, at this point we could have taken a short cut through built up areas to get to the harbour at St Ives, but chose to follow the official route which encircles The Island or St Ives Head and on round past Smeaton's Pier. There is much to delight the stroller in St Ives. It is a compact little seaside resort with its maze of narrow streets, interesting pubs and pleasant eating places, but on this occasion we were content to watch the world go by and enjoy a well earned cup of tea on the waterfront. The last 20 odd miles had been a hard slog.

Our walking plans for 1993 were hopefully to include the final leg of The Southwest Coast Path, unfortunately I'd developed a tyre round my middle and had trouble tying my shoelaces. I thought, "Goodness me, what am I turning into?" Most men of my age would order another bottle of Beaujolais and a fillet steak by way of consolation. I hoped to keep on walking.

My sister Delcie Manning who has lived and farmed in Devon with her husband Peter for the last thirty odd years had long expressed a wish to join Ruth and me on our ramble of the Coastal Path. This was the main reason to commence walking from the "Top end" of the path which starts at Minehead. Not that the Somerset and North Devon Path is an easy option, in fact it includes some of the most strenuous sections. For example just to the east of Combe Martin it rises to over 1000 feet above sea level.

13th March 1993
Minehead to Porlock Weir – 8 miles

On Minehead seafront halfway between the station and the harbour, just north of The Red Lion Hotel there is a prominent signpost proclaiming, "Coast Path to Poole 500 Miles." From personal experience Ruth and I can confirm that by "shanks pony" it certainly seems a long, long way. Guarded from traffic by black and white painted posts set firmly in the ground the official route sets off through an inconspicuous opening between two

Minehead. The end of the coastal path

cottages. This is an old donkey track which rises steeply through an attractive pine forest known as Culver Cliff Wood, although on this bright, cold mid-March day when our journey commenced everywhere was bare of greenery with undergrowth only just beginning to stir from its dormant winter shut down. Keeping parallel with the coast to pass above a small public garden the path zigzags steeply upwards to join a tarmac road on a hairpin bend. For a while we followed this narrow road through tall trees until the point where the coast path leaves the road and at this spot one is well above sea level. Eventually we came to a cairn marking the Exmoor National Park boundary with its distinctive deer head and antlers. Turning slightly inland we next reached the gorse and bracken covered top of North Hill. Burgundy Chapel Combe is deep and wide but thankfully the path swings inland to go around the headland keeping on the landward side of two long deserted farmhouses at West Myne and East Myne. On reaching the next

signpost with its welcoming acorn insignia with one arm pointing forward to Selworthy Beacon and Bossington whilst the right hand fork reads: "Rugged cliff top path to Hurlstone Point." Apparently this latter path is much more spectacular yet dangerous in gale force conditions. We chose to stay on the official route around Bossington Hill which wanders inland from Hurlstone Point. This is a laborious detour and unfortunately taking a wrong turning we ended up high above West Lynch completely lost in Allerford plantation. The only good point was that the woods were picturesque, finally after numerous arguments as to which path to take we succeeded in reaching Lynch to cross a swift flowing stream by a wooden bridge. From here a country lane lead us to Bossington Farm rejoining the path once more at Bossington Beach. We now had a hard tramp of two miles following the pebble ridge all the way to Porlock Weir. What a relief it was to find my brother-in-law patiently waiting to transport three weary hikers back to a hot bath, a log fire and a scrumptious evening meal, prepared by none other than Peter himself.

14th March 1993
Porlock Weir to Lynmouth Harbour – 12.75 miles

I find it surprising how a good nights sleep in a king size bed puts bounce back into seventy year old legs. Porlock Weir to Lynmouth Harbour is a gruelling 12.75 miles by the coastal path, yet despite yesterday's strenuous walk we were all raring to go.

At Porlock Weir the path goes behind the Anchor Hotel, through a bridle gate, along the side of a field behind red tile roofed houses, then over a stile keeping to the higher side of a large field, passing through a gate and at the far end joins a lane going west until reaching the decorative flint and brick arches of Worthy Combe Toll Lodge. Passing through the right hand arch one follows a pretty woodland path towards Culbone. From here on one follows red and yellow patches painted on stones or posts which mark the new route. After a while we came to a bridge crossing another footpath below and immediately after the bridge we turned sharp right to visit the tiny church at Culbone. Hidden away in a lonely combe, this medieval building is only 34 feet long by 12 feet wide and lays claim to being the smallest complete church in regular use anywhere in England. It has seats for just thirty people including a family size box pew. Shortly after leaving Culbone we found the path closed because of yet another landslip and a diversion inland. Although well signposted it was to add some three miles to our walk until joining the official path once more just north of Sugarloaf Hill. In my opinion the diversion was unnecessarily long and could be shortened considerably. At Broomstreet Farm the path passes through the farmyard before turning to keep parallel with the coast. Initially we followed a rough track until having reached a grassy field all sign of any path vanished. Passing through a gap in the earth bank at the lower end of the meadow we made a steep descent towards a gushing stream in the depths of Wheatham Combe. We were unfortunately too early in the year to see the wild combe at its best. A month later and the steep banks would be a riot of colour, decked with the blooms of rhododendrons, celendines, primroses and bluebells. Eventually climbing out of the combe we reached Yenworthy Wood, a weird place of stunted, twisted oak trees which struggle to survive in the rocky soil, whilst on these almost vertical cliff slopes the sea is some 650 feet below. After a while we emerged onto open meadows moving onto the point where the path keeps close to a stone bank field boundary and reaches a spot called Guildhall Corner. I could see no reason to connect this place in name with Guildhall Hall of Corporation city of London, used for state banquets etc. The path zigzags downwards whilst still high above the sea, moving westwards it follows a grass terrace then turns sharply inland before descending into Yenworthy Combe. In this area one combe follows another and the continuous descents and ascents make very tiring walking and slow progress. Wingate Combe was our next major obstacle and here the path goes way inland before crossing Wingate Stream then turning back on itself returns to the edge of the sea above Desolation Point. From here looking back eastwards one gets a good view of the Giant's Rib. A pair of natural archways; the scenery is beautiful beyond words. After crossing two more streams we passed Desolate Farm, a rundown place which certainly lives up to its name. With little scope for diversification I hope the hard working occupants get their fair share of E.E.C hand-outs going the rounds these days.

Continuing westwards, keeping parallel with the sea until rejoining the original path just east of Pudleep Gurt, (one of a series of rather impressive miniature gorges). It is a beautiful area with masses of greenery, ferns, mosses and many tiny waterfalls in this region of high rainfall. At this point we were still quite a few miles from Lynmouth and as one looks ahead at the mountainous scree covered slopes one gets the impression that the way ahead is impregnable. Passing the gully called Great Red we kept to the clifftop path along the edge of Butter Hill. From a view point near the top we got our first glimpse of Lynmouth some 3 miles across the bay. Continuing to climb, the grassy path crosses Wind Hill which on the day of our passing certainly lived up to its name, in fact my sister was very conscious of the danger of being blown over the cliff edge so strong was the wind. Opposite Countisbury Lodge Hotel the path starts a long descent in wide sweeping zigzags until finally emerging onto a beachside path leading straight to Lynmouth Harbour.

15th March 1993
Lynmouth to Hunter's Inn – 4 miles

From Lynmouth to Lynton the path winds upwards for almost 1000 feet. We had intended making use of the cliff railway but unfortunately with the summer season not yet underway it was not working. However, we cheated here somewhat hitching a lift by car to join the high level tarmac path called the North Walk which takes one very happily out to Castle Rock and Rugged Jack at Wringcliff Bay. Wild goats graze in this area and around the corner is the renowned Valley of Rocks. This is one of the finest pieces of coastal path in North Devon, and should not be missed by anyone who is reasonably sure-footed. The goats seem to be quite at home here, grazing on seemingly impossible slopes and on the narrowest of ledges hundreds of feet above the waves. Continuing westwards the path goes seawards into the woods, this track through the trees crosses a small bridge over a stream, finally coming out of Woody Bay Wood, past massive steep slopes leading up towards the Roman Fortlet, then around the next corner is Hollow Brook and a magnificent waterfall. So isolated is this beautiful spot that I am sure comparatively few people cast their eyes on this wonderland of nature. After some miles the path descends to the floor of the valley through which flows the river Heddon and here we diverted inland for half a mile to end our walk for the day and this session at the renowned Hunter's Inn.

13th April 1993
Hunter's Inn to Combe Martin – 9 miles

It was well into April '93 before time was found in our busy 'retired' lifestyle to continue our marathon walk. Our journey began on Friday 13th. One of those days my superstitious grandmother would have called a "Bad time for starting anything."

Leaving Hunter's Inn the path briefly follows the eastern bank of the river Heddon downstream until reaching a new footbridge to join a track on the other side. Strangely one now has to continue upstream again for quite a distance until one comes out of the woods and into a steep, dry valley covered in bracken, hawthorn and silver birch. From now on the coast path zigzags uphill in wide sweeps until reaching the 600 foot contour line, then swings back towards the sea to overlook the treacherous rocks at the mouth of

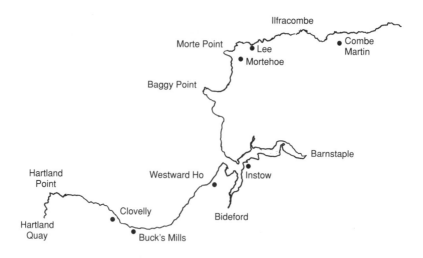

the river Heddon. Continuing west from Peter Rock the path is narrow, less than a yard wide in fact and follows the very steep upper slopes of the cliffs. It is a difficult section with outcrops of jagged slate and much loose scree underfoot but after yet another steep climb around East Cleave a magnificent view of the cliffs to the west opens up, with the heights of Trentishoe Down and Holdstone Down to the southwest. Each towering to over 1,000 feet above the sea. Luckily we did not have to reach the top of either of them!!

We traversed windswept Holdstone Down then followed the path well inland taking the tortuous route around the deep valley of Sherrycombe before approaching the heights of Girt Down. From now on it is uphill all the way as we made for a cairn way ahead which marks the summit of the Great Hangman. At 1043 feet it is the highest point on the South West Coastal Path, almost twice as high as Golden Cap on the Dorset coast. It had been a taxing slog for two old age pensioners like ourselves, but well worth the effort involved, for the view was sensational, like being on top of the world. On the summit we sat on a pile of stones to have our photograph taken. Proof that we had conquered our miniature Mount Everest. Surely there can be nothing ahead of us now to daunt us from our goal? Beyond and to the west lay the wide sweep of Combe Martin Bay with the view point of Little Hangman in the foreground. Following a grassy ridge we passed through a kissing gate, down some wooden steps, then alongside a wire fence round the back of Wild Pear Beach. A pretty spot with the clifftop a colourful garden of bluebells, primroses, violets, celandines and wood sage. We arrived in the village of Combe Martin at 5pm. In about six hours we had covered just 9 miles, certainly nothing to shout about but in our books we were very well pleased with our achievement.

14th April 1993
Combe Martin to Mortehoe – 13 miles

It is truly amazing how a good nights sleep revitalise tired bodies. The day after our triumph over the Great Hangman we set off from Combe Martin on what was to prove the toughest 13 miles of the whole path. Certainly this was so in my case, we walked and climbed almost non stop for 9 hours, thrice climbing from sea level to 650 feet plus many lesser climbs. After Ilfracombe the path is especially strenuous. A deep wooded valley leads down to Lee Bay, a sheltered cove, with its tiny village and large hotel. Clumps of fuchsias and hydrangeas contribute dashes of rich colour and seaweed draped rocks are all that is left of the beach at high tide. Then there is the climb out of Lee Bay to Bull Point and a long, long drag out to Morte Point, a wild, untamed promontory battered continuously by giant waves.

A glance at the map will show how Morte Point juts out into the Atlantic, but it is well worth a visit to this view point. Making our way cautiously over huge, jagged slabs of blue-grey rock and round the Point, the coast of Wales disappears from view, and in exchange, virtually the whole of the rest of North Devon's coastline stretched away as far as the eye could see.

Our time spent at Morte Point was brief, the sun was already getting low over the Atlantic, it would have been great to have stopped awhile and seen the sun set, but time did not allow. I had arranged with Peter that we would be at Mortehoe awaiting collection at 5pm.

This walk from Combe Martin had been a tough one, it was already 6 o'clock and we still had two more miles to go. I knew my brother-in-law would be worried to death that we had met with some great calamity on this lonely coastline. All three of us were thankful that the last two miles to Mortehoe was downhill all the way, otherwise I don't think I could have made it. I was really shattered and my two companions were on their last legs as we staggered, tired and weary into Mortehoe. Thankfully, Peter was still patiently waiting. "What kept you? You are three hours late, I quite thought you had all fallen into the sea and been swept away." "Come on, lets get home, I want my supper, I'm starving," said Peter with undisguised relief.

15th/16th April 1993
Mortehoe to Barnstable – 20 miles

We took two days to complete this section. It could have been walked in less time of course but we were in no desperate hurry, finding enjoyment in the ever changing scenery. Apart from the gentle climb out to Baggy Point it is mainly flat walking all the way, and whilst we prefer the wild, lonely cliff scenery it made a pleasant change and of course was far less tiring. From Woolacombe we made our way across the sandy, surf pounded beach that sweeps southwards for 2 miles until reaching the car park, here upon making a right angled turn we climbed Napps Cliff then followed a manure strewed cattle path along the high slope out to Baggy Point. From this spot on the mainland you can enjoy one of the closest views of Lundy Island and beyond, the high cliffs of Pembrokeshire and the Gower peninsular. In a few more miles we rounded Croyde Bay then following the B3231 we reached Saunton Sands.

Backed by Braunton Burrows, this huge expanse of sand runs southwards for more than 3 miles to Crow Point, off which the waters of the Taw and Torridge meet the Atlantic. From behind the hotel we picked up the bridle path which winds and twists through sand dunes and thickets. This desolate area is not only a National Nature Reserve but also includes the golf course and the Ministry of Defence firing range. Our route took us to the rear of the golf course until finally arriving at the mouth of the river Taw.

At the most southern point of Braunton Marsh it is less than a thousand yards across the river Taw to dry land on the other side, but there is no way to cross and no ferry. To walk from the point to Instow via Barnstable is 20 miles around the estuary. 20 miles to advance 1000 yards! One can of course catch a bus in Braunton and be driven round in comfort for about £2 each. We chose to walk, not I may add to save money but so as not to miss out on a complete change of scenery.

The coast path now continues east along a wide stone track with low marshy meadows on the left and bramble covered dunes on the right. Passing the White House the path runs along the grassy top of the sea wall besides the estuary all the way to Braunton, (six and a half miles away). As I have mentioned before no two sections of the Coastal Path are the same, there is always something different to see or hear and we certainly did! Since leaving Saunton we had been accompanied by the ceaseless roar of jet engines from aircraft taking off and landing at the nearby Chivenor Air Station. Where the path follows the estuary in a wide sweeping curve modern Tornado jets came in on their landing approach so close above our heads that we had a clear view of the two occupants. Whilst on the parallel runway planes of the Red Arrows were taking off in groups of three, banking sharply over the downs to give anyone interested a free demonstration of their skills. Following the seawall past the Old Toll House, on reaching Velator T-junction we turned right making our way along the redundant railway. Finally through a decrepit white gate opposite the grandstand at Barnstable R.F.C, we walked up a narrow lane taking the right-hand fork into Mill Lane, coming out onto Rolle Quay. From here it was only a few hundred yards to our parked car in which we had left the necessary ingredients to brew a much needed cup of tea!!

17th April 1993
Barnstable to Westward Ho! – 9 miles

Where Rudyard Kipling went to school so I've been told.

The distance is measured walking from Barnstable to Instow, using the ferry across to Appledore then walking on to Westward Ho! Unfortunately the ferry is seasonal and also subject to tide. We were out of luck, the ferry wasn't working this meant yet another long detour inland to cross the river Torridge by the magnificent new road bridge. Crossing the bridge must be done with care, traffic is heavy and there is no footpath access. Arriving safely in Bideford we followed The Southwest Coastal Path through a mainly built up area to Appledore but forked off left past Knapp House to round Bloody Corner before reaching Westward Ho! I tried to find out the reason for this unusual place name but without success. Probably relates to some desperate skirmish between customs men and a smuggling gang in days gone by.

22nd May 1993
Buck's Mills to Westward Ho! and Appledore – 10 miles
Plus Buck's Mills to Hartland Quay – 14 miles

These are very fine sections indeed. What coastal path walking is all about but be warned it is strenuous to say the least, especially around Clovelly. It took us two days. The first day leaving our car at Appledore, we took a taxi to Buck's Mills with the plan of walking back to Westward Ho! However I reckoned we were ripped off, there was no meter in his private vehicle and he charged £15 for a 20 minute journey. Perhaps he hoped that his horror stories told on the way about the dangers of elderly people walking the coast path would make us change our minds and ask to be driven back again!

Nestling in a wooded valley, Buck's Mills amounts to little more than one narrow street, hemmed in by whitewashed cottages, which runs for half a mile from a small car park to the sea. Tree clad cliffs rise up behind a pebbled, sand-patched beach where the ebbing tide leaves many interesting rock pools. We left Buck's Mills at 10.20 am not an early start for the long day's walk ahead of us. It's a stiff climb out of the village the path begins a series of ups and downs which escalates, each climb becoming steeper than the last. We hadn't made very good time and it was 4 pm by the time we reached Westward Ho! Declining the easy option of making for Appledore through the built up area we kept to the sea-shore walking on the pebble ridge which circles Northam Burrows Country Park and the Sandymere golf course and what a long hard slog that was. The huge grey pebbles are impossible to walk on and to make matters worse it came on to rain with wind reaching gale force blowing unchecked across Bideford Bay. The route (there is no path as such) seems to go on and on for ever following a low level coastline that looks the shape of a baboon's face on the map. We had reached the end of our tether as we rounded the mudflats of the Skern and the outskirts of Appledore. My blistered feet throbbed, my legs ached and it seemed they were about to call a strike at any moment. Yet once in the shelter of houses we seemed to get 'second wind.' Forgetting how cold and wet we were as we walked the whole length of Irsha Street, Old Appledore, where every house is painted in bright colours and each one differs from it's neighbour. Checking carefully as we past down the street I couldn't find any two identical.

23rd May 1993
Buck's Mills to Hartland Quay – 14 miles

The section of the path we walked today was from Buck's Mills to Hartland Quay via Clovelly and Hartland Point. Approximately

14 miles of what is perhaps the most scenic of the Somerset and North Devon Coast Path. My sister Delcie accompanied Ruth and me on this section bringing along two of her friends Robert and Jackie Rose. Our small party had the advantage of Robert's Range Rover for the day which meant that with my car we had a vehicle at both ends of the proposed walk. Back to Buck's Mills for the second time in two days our new companions wanted a coffee break before the hike even began! Luckily the village boasts a small shop which sells tea, coffee, ice creams and delicious hot pastries. On the way down to the beach there are toilets and a drinking water tap, two essentials for ramblers, the trouble I found with toilet facilities in out of the way places is that in times of dire need eight months out of the year they are more than likely to be securely locked up. My pet solution to this problem was to nip round the back of the building where the state of the undergrowth indicated I was not the only one with the same idea. From the seaward side of the shop a small pathway leads west. Stone steps rise into Buck's Wood where a narrow track winds steadily upwards to emerge next to some old disused, stone farm buildings. Turning due west we followed a track until reaching Walland Cary a stately home now used as a holiday camp. We continued on our way following a sunken road through a beautiful beech wood, the overhanging branches just bursting into their full summer foliage creating a tunnel-like effect. We just had to get snapping with our camera. After crossing a large field and climbing over yet another stile the path dropped down to a bridge over a small stream, then climbing out of this pretty valley we quickly reached Hobby Drive. This nineteenth century roadway created for some wealthy gentleman to drive his horse and carriage around his estate makes a pleasant 3 mile stroll along the coast to Clovelly.

This unique Devon fishing village with its single stone cobbled street drops steeply to the tiny harbour and draws thousands of visitors each year. Coaches and motor cars deposit camera clicking tourists in untold numbers at the hilltop vehicle park from where they sally forth down a narrow zigzag lane to reach the one and only street. Just a few of the more energetic arrive by pedal cycle but few, precious few indeed have walked like we have along the coastal path from Minehead over 100 hilly miles away!!

Quaint whitewashed cottages bright with flowers flank each side of the narrow street whilst proprietors of the many souvenir shops, ice cream parlours and tea rooms strive to lighten visitors pockets for their return journey. A journey that until recently could be made on the backs of weary donkeys. These days it seems do-gooders have succeeded in getting these overworked animals early retirement to pastures green. Now for something like 60p per head one can get a lift to the top by a back road behind the village in a long wheelbase Landrover.

We spent two hours in Clovelly in fact Jackie and Robert although they now dwell in Devon had never visited the village before. This often happens. One tours the world looking for one knows not what and fails to visit beauty spots on one's doorstep. We broke our strict rule in Clovelly, wasting daylight hours by stopping at a coffee shop for refreshments, not a sensible thing to do considering we had eleven miles of hard walking to reach Hartland Quay before dark, but I'm afraid our new companions lacked the experience of coastal path walking. Besides we were carrying ample rations anyway.

We left Clovelly by a narrow path which takes one north-westwards from the harbour up and through the garden of a delightful little cottage, literally within feet of the occupants front door. Up and up, what a climb it was, few come this way: most tourists take the easy option and fork out their 60 pence for Landrover transportation to the top. We followed a rough path through the woods until reaching a small field, at the far end of which was a kissing gate. Now Jackie, an attractive red-head who hails from the States failed to understand that a kissing gate refers to its construction and nothing more. She seemed to think that the name had something to do with showing affection to the 'trip organiser', or so she said! Whereupon she gave me a bear-hug and proceeded to plant kisses on my weather beaten features.

Shortly after this hilarious distraction the sea view vanished as the path dipped down into a long, dark tunnel of rhododendrons. For the next mile or so the path ran parallel to the steeply sloping cliff top, passing through dense woodland and overgrown gorse, climbing steadily all the while. Suddenly, we emerged at the top of an almost sheer cliff. Gallantry Bower 325 feet above the sea, so named because the story goes that in the past loving couples who had been forbidden to marry jumped to their doom from this cliff locked in each others arms. Westwards from Gallantry Bower the path clings precariously to the cliff top giving one an excellent view of Blackchurch Rock with its two natural archways carved by the relentless pounding of the waves. Rounding a huge rock a set of steps headed off the main path, we decided to explore. They lead down and through a dark tunnel to a summer house, stone built with a green painted door and a superb view of the coastline. From the weathering of the stones I guessed at least two centuries had past since some maiden had meditated at this lonely yet beautiful spot. From this point we followed a steep and dangerous path which descended to eventually rejoin the official path at Mouth Mill. It had been well worth this diversion. On reaching Windbury Waterfall – an exquisite spot for a picnic – by a unanimous vote all agreed on a refreshment stop. I generously allowed a thirty minute respite before climbing Windbury Head at 468 feet a lonely, windswept headland with prehistoric earthworks. Beyond, there were no more major cliffs to surmount until we reached Hartland Point some four miles ahead. On this section we were all spell-bound by what is perhaps the wildest uninhabited coastline in England with shadowy coves and great buttresses at whose feet the gale-lashed Atlantic waves pound relentlessly. Apart from a track that leads out to the lighthouse on Hartland Point no roads reach the isolated bays which means the area is seldom visited by the general public who usually make a bee-line for the B&B's and caravan sites near sandy beaches where ice creams, the tea shop and Chinese take-aways are close at hand.

We had been walking since 10 am, it was now 6 pm and we still had a three mile hard slog ahead of us. The coast path continues southwest following the cliff tops. Ahead Damehole Point and Gull Rock stand out prominently, with a strange, wild, hanging valley behind called Smoothlands, the valley floor dotted with clumps of heather, gorse, bracken and really giant anthills. We made good use of some thoughtfully placed stepping stones over a very marshy spot before climbing out of the valley to get our first view of Stoke Church Tower. But the view didn't last for long as the path drops down steeply at this point to Blegberry Water with its sparkling waterfall, only to rise almost vertically to the top of a sheer slab of rock 650 feet above the sea. Our physical resources were rapidly diminishing yet shortly we found ourselves faced by the challenge of hurling ourselves up yet another killer slope. By the time we reached Hartland Quay the sun had long set. For us it had been one of the hardest and longest coastal path walks to date. We were all shattered to say the least.

25th May 1993
Hartland Quay to Morwenstow – 6 miles

Hartland Quay: Three of England's most famous sailors – Sir Francis Drake, Sir Walter Raleigh and Sir John Hawkins – financed the building of a small harbour here in the 16th century. Providing a welcome refuge on this inhospitable part of the Devon coast. The little bay is backed by impressive cliffs whose layers of rock go from horizontal to vertical in the space of a few yards. On this section of our walk Delcie, Ruth and myself were again favoured by the company of Robert and Jackie. We had all recovered remarkable well from the previous day's marathon walk. Unfortunately heavy thunderstorms had struck the area during the night, the ground was waterlogged and still it rained cats and dogs as the saying goes. With a force 8 gale blowing off the Atlantic my companions were all for calling the walk off. "For goodness sake." I said, "it's only a bit of rain and the wind is behind us," "You'll not melt." As my mother would have said. I had my way, but secretly I had doubts whether it had been the right decision. Besides having to cope with inclement weather the guide book warned that this was a very tough section and would surely take much longer than planned. Initially the path is no more than a grassy track passing behind St Catherine's Tor, then you cross a stream on some round concrete stepping stones, before climbing up, then down again to the dramatic waterfall at Speke's

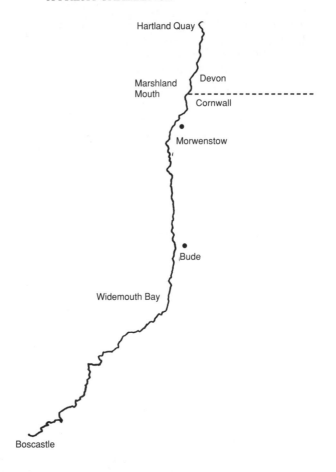

Mill Mouth, a lovely spot where wild iris grow in perfusion. It is a long haul from the base of the waterfall to Mansley Cliff but once at the top the view stretches west for miles along a chain of uninhabited bays and headlands. The cliffs and rockwalls were covered in spring flowers, a riot of colour. Pinks, and reds and yellows, a natural garden the like of which cannot be recreated even with a regiment of hard-working gardeners. Only by walking the coastal path can this wonderland be discovered.

26th May1993, the day of a review of the fleet to commemorate victory in the battle of the Atlantic 50 years previous. A significant day for the Royal Navy and for Ruth and me, a sort of milestone on our long distance walk, this was the day we crossed the border from England to Cornwall. Readers of my adventures should know that Cornish people mention they don't live in England. Having dropped down to sea level, at this point we made use of the conveniently placed stepping stones to cross Marsland Water, the spot which marks the Devon / Cornish border. 112 miles from Minehead round the coastline. From now on we were following the North Cornwall Coastal Path, I checked my compass, we were heading southwest. Was it my imagination or could I really smell the aroma of fish and chips coming in on the prevailing wind from St Ives!

From the top of Marsland Cliff the path crosses two deep combes before reaching Henna Cliff from where we struck inland to Morwenstow Church. This ancient building sheltered by wind bent trees is well worth a visit. A number of shipwrecked seafarers are buried in the churchyard it is also well known for its 19th century vicar the late Reverend R. S. Hawker, and another point worth considering is that refreshments are available at the old Rectory!

26th August 1993
Morwenstow to Bude – 5 miles

Since we were last at Morwenstow the summer months had slipped by, it was now late August. Once again my sister had expressed a keen desire to join forces with Ruth and me. She seemed quite bitten by the long distance walking bug, yet try as she might she was still unable to convince her husband Peter of the long term benefits to be gained. He pooh-poohed the idea that he would lose weight and feel fitter within the week. He stuck steadfast to his considered opinion that we were all quite mad! Leaving the church the coastal path strikes out diagonally across a grass field to Vicarage Cliff and the magnificent view point on Higher Sharpnose Point. On this section a National Trust sign reads 'Hawker's Hut.' It is easily missed if you don't keep your eyes open. Built right on the cliff edge you go down a few steps and there you will see a hut nestling under sea-thrift and stonecrop and giving a superb view out to sea. Hawker, the vicar of Morwenstow for forty years built his hut of driftwood and apparently used it as a place of meditation whilst writing poetry and occasionally enjoying an opium pipe. The path westwards to Bude is mainly at a high level with a number of deep combes especially the one at Steeple Point where the official path is most spectacular. Contour lines on our ordnance survey are at 10 metre vertical intervals and in this area are shown so close on our map that they almost run together making for some stiff climbs. This walk is not for anyone without a good head for heights. To make matters worse bad weather set in, it came on to rain, really throwing it down. Ruth had the bright idea to cut the bottom open of three black plastic dustbin bags which we always carried to sit on at lunchtime if the ground was wet. Stepping into them we then tied the bags at the waist with baler twine, (you don't catch a farmer without a knife and a good length of twine). This plan worked well preventing our trousers and long socks getting saturated as water ran in cascades off our macs. For a while we pressed on regardless, heading into the wind driven rain but finally faced with a particularly high level, open cliff to cross we were forced to seek shelter in a small cave. To restore energy and inject a little enthusiasm for another battle with the elements we shared a Mars bar. Half an hour later the clouds broke, the sun came out and our spirits rose with the temperature. The coastal path took us alongside the Composite Signals Organisation Station at Cleave Camp where massive satellite tracing dish aerials dominate the scene. Passing the boundary fence of this establishment we pressed on along the gorse covered cliff top. It wasn't long after this that we dropped down to the shelter of the very popular Duckpool Beach. Well worth a visit if only to dip your toes in the water. Walking south from Duckpool the path climbs in a wide zigzag sweep to the top of Warren Point before dropping yet again to Warren Gutter a most interesting area where huge rock formations are exposed, standing almost horizontal out of the water. From now on to Bude there are numerous sandy beaches but bathing can be dangerous, particularly at low tide when the coastal currents can be very strong. Not that we wished to bathe, we were wet enough already!

27th August 1993
Boscastle Harbour to Crackington Haven – 7 miles

We walked this section in reverse so to speak walking north-east. Because we were getting so far down the Cornish coastline we moved camp to B & B with Rachel and Chris Crooker. Tregather Farm, Crackington Haven. They proved to be a most hospitable family and after we had enjoyed a real farmhouse breakfast Rachel insisted she drove us to Boscastle Harbour for the start of our walk to Crackington Haven. Boscastle with its tiny harbour guarded by Meachard Island and Penally Point is an interesting village of thatched, limewashed cottages. It also boasts three pubs: The Wellington, The Cobweb and The Napoleon. They all have a welcoming appearance but I can't vote on the quality of the beer. I was gently steered past all three!

One starts the walk on a very steep climb up Penally Hill and it was not long before we came to Pentargon where a stream empties onto the beach in a spectacular 120 foot waterfall. Following the cliff top past Seals Hole and Fire Beacon Point with The Beeny Sisters, dangerous, semi submerged rocks immediately below. Next, just out to sea is Gull Rock followed by Buckator, a sheer black cliff with white bands of quartz running through it. Shortly, with some relief we dropped down to a little sandy beach so isolated and inaccessible that I'm sure few members of the public know of its existence, not another human being in sight, not even a boat at sea, or plane overhead. We stayed an hour sitting on a rock with our blistered toes immersed in the sea and enjoyed some light refreshments from our back packs. But much as we would have liked we couldn't stay all day, there was some strenuous walking to be done before reaching Crackington Haven. The path now begins the ascent of High Cliff, a superb view point owned by the National Trust from which Lundy Island, more than 30 miles away, can by seen on a clear day. Towering 731 feet above the sea, it is the highest cliff in Cornwall and one of the highest anywhere on England's coastline. Once we had this climb under our belts surely I felt there could be nothing else to prevent us completing the whole course! We pressed on keeping to high ground as the next section can be dangerous if one gets too low and onto loose scree or slate slabs. By-passing The Strangles – a small sandy beach – we walked right out to Cambeak Point before turning due east and following the cliff top path to Crackington, just seven miles from Boscastle but it had taken us all day. It is my considered opinion that Cornish miles are much longer than ours back home.

28th August 1993
Crackington Haven To Bude – 12 miles

This section can surprise the unwary and before you have finished it you will really know in no uncertain fashion that you have had a tough walk! This is wildest Cornwall at its most spectacular best. The weather had closed in overnight. Heavy drizzle and dense sea mist swept inland off the Atlantic as we set of for Bude. We had enjoyed a typical farmhouse breakfast at Tregather House but since this homely B & B is set well back from the coast we had to make our way blindly across fields for over a mile to pick up the coastal path. I said a silent prayer on the way, trusting that 'He' was watching, would take pity and prevent us from stumbling over a cliff edge when we reached our destination.

One point of interest, especially to Ruth and me was that just before reaching the path despite the poor visibility we discovered a large natural cattle shelter. A deep depression in the land surface the size of a football pitch was covered in dense blackthorn and scrub trees, here away from the elements cattle were sheltering. It was obviously a spot favoured and used for centuries by the smallholder's cattle that grazed the rough pasture of the cliff tops. The almighty did watch over us. We reached Crackington Haven safely. Sat on a bench and had our coffee before leaving the village by the side of a lovely thatched cottage with a most picturesque garden, then up the hill on the long haul to Pencannow Point which rises to more than 400 feet above the waves. Parts of this walk are most strenuous with extremely deep combes to negotiate. In places the ascents are amongst the steepest on the whole of the Southwest Path especially the one up from Dizzard Point and another at Millook. Luckily, as the day wore on the weather improved, our morale rose quickly as the afternoon sun dried out our so-called 'waterproofs' however it was close on four o'clock by the time we dropped down to Widemouth Sand where we ate the last of our sandwiches sitting on a picnic bench outside a rundown beach cafe. Feeling guilty making use of the establishments seating capacity whilst eating our own food I rather foolishly purchased three plastic cups of very wishy washy lukewarm tea. We made this refreshment stop a short one, it was getting late in the day and we still had over 4 miles of walking before reaching Bude, besides the holiday makers crowding the beach made us appreciate the solitude of the lonely cliffs and hidden combes, those deep, seaward running valleys with their goblin woods and sheltered banks a perfect counterpoint to the wind swept coast. Far out from civilisation one gets the feeling that the path is your own, we didn't wish for intrusions, if the fancy took us we could sit and watch the sun go down.

31st August 1993
Trebarwith Strand to Boscastle – 7.5 miles – 135 miles from Minehead

The fantastic dry spell continued which made ideal weather conditions for walking.

From our B & B base at Tregather House we drove our car to Boscastle and paid £1.30 to park it for the day. The previous

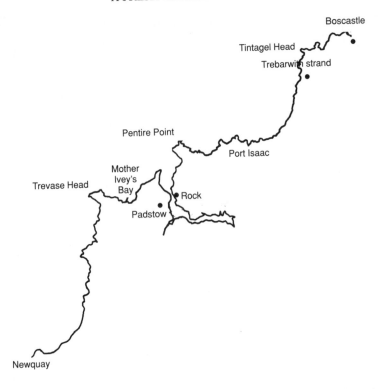

evening I had booked a taxi cab from Boscastle to take us along the coast road to Trebarwith Strand, the driver, a chatty Cornishman arrived at the appointed time of 10.15 am. The short journey cost me £8, but well worth the money, we couldn't expect our hard-working hosts to chauffeur us around the countryside everyday. This was another section that we walked the opposite way. It proved to be strenuous walking but very beautiful especially through the rugged, Rocky Valley. Walking eastwards from Trebarwith the many small, sandy beaches are submerged at high tide. It is a wild landscape with crumbling cliffs which were once quarried for slate but is now a paradise for seabirds. After passing The Sisters and Saddle Rock, dark, perilous and forboding, rocks just offshore that must have claimed a lot of ships in their time we

118

took turns in focusing our one and only pair of binoculars to watch the bird life on Long Island and the much smaller Short Island. The coast path now overlooked a deep, inaccessible cove with cliffs rising sheer out of the sea a feeding area for puffins. In all our previous travels I had never seen so many, apparently this is the largest puffin colony in Cornwall. Half an hour later we decided that it was time for our first refreshment stop of the day. What better spot than to sit on the cliff top high above 'Ladies Window', a natural archway on the western side of a small headland, as an added attraction there were grey seals feeding in the deep water far below. We had not seen another human being since setting out from Trebarwith. It was all very pleasant having the place to ourselves and in a way I must admit to feeling sorry for all those hardworking city folk in their 9 to 5 jobs and those that have to do battle with motorway traffic everyday. Unfortunately we were not making much forward progress we had dawdled, hypnotized by the desolate scenery and abundant bird life. Down now, down into the depth of Grower Gut, a steep rocky valley below Welltown. Reaching the bottom we crossed a swift flowing stream by gingerly stepping on algae covered granite blocks, if you don't slip you reach the other side dry!

We were now passing 'The Island' on which stands the gaunt ruins of a Celtic monastery which has stood on this spot since the dark ages. Nearly 300 steps, some of which are treacherous when wet take walkers to the top of The Island. Crowds of day trippers here, but much as we would have liked we couldn't spare the time to visit. There is always another day we consoled ourselves. We made our way through a miniature gorge where the coast path continues keeping close to the cliff edge, too close for comfort in some places, and all the while far below one hears the pounding of the Atlantic rollers on the rock defences. We didn't walk out to the Bronze Age fort on Willapark but cut straight across this promontory with its ancient strip field systems on our landward side. Headlands on the North Cornish coast are usually wild, weather-torn places yet are surprisingly rich in plant and wildlife, many species finding a niche between sea level and the wind blown clifftop. We eventually reached Boscastle at 6 pm pleasantly weary and with protesting leg muscles, however it had been a grand walk. It goes without saying that by now we had worked up a tremendous appetite which was later appeased at the Cobweb Inn. A pub with a long sea-faring history, and excellent beer. One I thoroughly recommend.

1st September 1993
Trebarwith Strand to Port Isaac – 7.5 miles

Today, weather brilliant, warm, sunny with a light breeze off the sea which makes for excellent walking conditions. Just as well since our guide book classifies this section as severe and although it is only 7 or 8 miles by coastal path the experts suggest one should allow 5 hours to complete the course. We were not out to break records. It took us 7 hours!

We were on our way by 9.30 am, leaving Trebarwith by following the coastal path to the landward side of the Port William public house then off to the left on a zig-zagging track uphill until finally reaching the top of Dennis Point. We had risen from sea level to the 300 foot contour line in 30 minutes and were about to drop to sea level once more at Backways Cove. This roller coaster footpath continued all day, in fact there are five steep drops and rises similar to the one we had just tackled before one finally reaches Port Isaac.

From the cliff top at Dennis Point we descended into a beautiful, secluded valley where a stream trickles into Backways Cove. Then we were faced with yet another severe climb to the top of Treligga Cliff. In a mile or so we passed 'The Mountain', a steep peak behind Tregardock Beach that has been isolated by erosion. Now the path passes disused lead and silver shafts to continue desperately close to the cliff edge and I would advise anyone without a head for height not to attempt this section. We were lucky there was no gale blowing on this day. At Jacket's Point the coast path descends once more to sea level and what a descent, almost a vertical drop. Icepicks would have been more useful than

The almost vertical path ahead taken from Jacket's Point

our walking sticks in fact Ruth was so scared of falling and rolling into the sea that she sat on her backside and inched her way downwards with the utmost caution, stay in bottom gear Ruth was my advice to her. We finally reached the old fishing village of Port Isaac at about 5 o'clock leaving ourselves enough time to explore the little harbour with its boats, nets and lobster pots which lies at the foot of steep slopes lined with thatched, whitewashed cottages. The streets are so narrow in some places that there is only just enough room for a car to thread between the buildings. One passage, called Sqeezibelly Alley, only 18 inches wide even poses problems for stout pedestrians! To Ruth and me, thankfully it caused no impediment. By now having walked over 500 miles across often difficult terrain on a rather sparse diet we could almost pass through two abreast!

2nd September 1993
Port Isaac to Rock – 12 miles

Still our luck held with the weather. Everyday the sun shone out of a cloudless sky. We were getting quite a suntan and another plus was that we could walk lightly clothed and even lightly shod. Out of Port Isaac one follows the public footpath starting at the foot of the narrow street which climbs out of the town on the southside of the harbour. From here the path rounds Lobber Point and then slopes down to Pine Haven. Rising to the cliff top, next it crosses Varley Head to continue its switchback way round Kellan Head and the Coastguard lookout, a truly dramatic stretch then on to Portquin. This tiny hamlet lies at the back of the inlet where low cliffs embrace a beach of shingle and low tide sand. To us it seemed a dreary backwater, apparently dwindling pilchard shoals caused near desertion of the village back in the middle of the nineteenth century. Having no desire to explore further we continued on our way until reaching the viewpoint on Doyden Point then on to Trevan Point where a refreshment break was taken. Now I must explain that lunch break on our coastal path walk was always an austere meal consisting of one small sandwich, perhaps an apple or an orange and a gill of lemon juice. The magnificent scenery was our feast. The landscape now had changed, the cliffs were not so high and the countryside had become gentler with kinder grazing land for stock. Having now entered National Trust Land the path is maintained in excellent condition and in addition, to restrain the farm livestock from the path and the cliff edge was a post and rail fence that could be described as nothing less than a work of art. Consisting of stout posts with four rails topped by a strand of barbed wire it faithfully followed the twisting coastline for two and a half miles. It must have cost a small fortune to erect in such rocky ground but it is certainly a job well done and I congratulate the craftsmen who erected it. After Carnweather Point a signpost pointed towards Rumps Point this was well worth the detour. One can clearly see the outline of Rumps Point Cliff castle, a fortified settlement of the Iron Age. A triple rampart across the neck of the headland defends access but of course did not prevent Ruth and me reaching the very point of this isolated place, which also gives one a good view of the little island of Newland to the west and The Mouls to the east. Except for these two specks of land there is only the Atlantic Ocean between here and America. There was not another soul in sight, we seemed to have this part of the Cornish coastline to ourselves. By now we were getting weary but plodded on, reaching Pentire Point which provides perhaps the best all round viewpoint of anywhere on the entire length of the Southwest Way. After rounding Pentire Point the path turns south almost doubling back on itself and it was now a gentle slope down hill all the way to the golden wave washed sands of New Polzeath. We took off our walking boots and two pairs of socks to paddle across the beach. The cool saltwater of the incoming tide did wonders for our protesting feet. Now followed a long stretch of relatively easy walking on the fine turf promenade known as The Greenway as far as Trebetherick Point then after skirting the golf course we entered the forbidding Sand Dunes. Now I have a slight idea of what it must be like to be lost in the Sahara Desert. Although the sun was getting low in the west it still gave off plenty of heat, we had no food left, or any drink and furthermore we were lost! I had never seen such huge sand dunes, some towered 100 – 150 feet above us. Thrice we followed a dead end trail that only lead to the base of a mountain of sand or the edge of the estuary and the incoming tide. I can vouch to the fact that walking on loose sand is very tiring especially at the end of a twelve mile hike. At that point in time I was willing to barter half my farm for a reliable camel! Somehow, in due course we made our way through to emerge at the car park for the River Camel ferry (foot passengers only). Just another half a mile on a firm pavement led us to the small town of Rock where we managed to catch the last bus back to Port Isaac.

3rd September 1993
Trevone to Padstow – 6 miles

We reluctantly took our leave of Chris and Rachel Crooker our B&B hosts at Tregather House which by the way I had learnt was part of Trevigue Farm, a 500 acre holding on which Chris kept sheep and milked a herd of 150 friesian cows, reminiscent of home I thought. It was at such times on our walk of the coastal path that a car was a boon. We had to reach the other side of the river Camel which meant driving inland to cross at Wadebridge. Driving to Trevone we booked for a two night stay at Mrs Staker, 'Sea winds' a tiny bungalow built almost on the beach. By the time we had moved to our new 'base camp' and had some lunch it was one o'clock. Nevertheless we decided on what was for us a short walk of some six miles out to the Daymark on Stepper Point then along the side of the Camel Estuary to finish at North Quay in Padstow.

The grandeur of Mother Ivey's Bay

4th September 1993.
Porthcothan to Trevone – 7 miles

The everlasting problem for those walking everyday is how to return to your vehicle or B & B base. One way or the other we seemed to have got ourselves from A to B without too much difficulty. With the hospitality we had come to expect from the Cornish people our host kindly drove us in her car to Porthcothan from where we set off for Trevone via Trevose Head. The path follows a zigzag course along a very broken coastline but once on the cliff top it is relatively easy walking. Reaching the wide expanse of fine sand at Booby's Bay and Constantine Bay at low tide we marched briskly across the sandy beach before being forced to climb the cliff to reach Dinas Head. In this area is 'Stinking Cove.' What a sweet name! But with Cat's Cove just around the corner perhaps there is some connection. We stopped briefly in Mother Ivey's Bay. The place looked dead, there was no sign of a shop or an ice cream van and the only habitation seemed to be Mother Ivey's Cottage. I expect we would have been made welcome if I had tapped on the door and asked for a cup of tea, but couldn't pluck up enough courage to do so. We didn't look very presentable in our walking gear, so we made do with a fruit and nut chocolate bar which provided enough energy to reach our destination for the day. Porthcothan proved to be our furthest point west on the north coast of Cornwall for 1993.

Porthcothan to St. Ives – 52 miles in total

My sister Delcie was back, she had elected to join Ruth and me on the last lap of our marathon coastal path walk. Now just a mere 52 miles to go, fortunately most of the three million tourists who swarm over the Cornish peninsular every year make a bee-line for the popular seaside resorts, such as Newquay, Penzance or St Ives, and so leave room in the quieter, lovelier places, even in high summer. But I recommend spring and autumn. In spring, especially, the mild gulf stream brings the flowers early. To savour Cornwall, leave your car and walk the coastal path. Your senses will swim from the scent of flowers, the glint of sunshine through the trees, the constant changing sky. Stand on those mighty cliffs, gaze out to sea, and dream.

24th April 1994
Portcothan to Mawgan Porth – 7 miles

Porthcothan: A stream flows into the sea at the head of this long, narrow inlet, where shingle-speckled sand is backed by a small area of low dunes. Suitably clad and with morale high we set off westwards climbing on a sandy track and making for the clifftop. It was grand to be back, this is another wild stretch of coast carved by

Bedruthan Steps

the elements into a series of eroded inlets and jutting headlands and a coastline of many rocky islands just off shore, a danger to inshore shipping either accidental or in the old days lured to destruction by unscrupulous wreckers. We descended into a deep gully to cross a stream by means of a wooden footbridge, the sea birds and seals have these isolated coves to themselves. Ahead, a long climb to the next clifftop then around High Cove and out to the sharp point of Park Head where one gets a good view of two tiny islands called Cow and Calf, but for the life of me I couldn't see the slightest resemblance to any of our bovine stock back at the farm. Park Head is often referred to as the Land's End of North Cornwall. Many trippers visit this spot, they mostly come by car, walk a little then go away, they should venture further. We did just that, explored the towering cliffs for a few more miles until discovering Bedruthan Steps. A long flight of slippery and extremely steep steps

127

plunging down from the grassy cliff top to a dramatic beach where low-tide sands are punctuated by immense rocks. Legend has it that the rocks were stepping stones used by the giant Bedruthan. More truthfully they are granite stacks left isolated on the beach by erosion of softer rocks around them. But it makes a nice fairy story. Finding a sheltered spot in the lea of Queen Bess Rock we tucked into our refreshments, whilst listening to the huge Atlantic rollers break on the beach and contemplating the long climb out of this fantastic cove. Two hours later rounding a sandy river estuary we reach Mawgan Porth and decided to call it a day. That evening we dined well at the Pheasant Inn in Newlyn East. This usually quiet country pub was crowded out on this particular evening. Film crews with their paraphernalia had moved into the village ready for an early start next day on the new film series, 'Wycliffe', starring Jack Sheppard as the dour Cornish copper. A series that is hoped will do for Cornwall what Bergerac did for Jersey.

25th April 1994
Mawgan Porth to Newquay and The Gannel – 7 miles

It was a squally morning as we left Mawgan Porth beach by the side of the cafe and beach shop. Past a pair of coast guard cottages then up a sandy incline to reach the cliff top only to head into a howling, force 8 gale which whipped and tore at our waterproofs and headgear forcing us to bend almost double to make forward progress, but then bad weather brings a new relish with gales and cold comprising worthwhile adversaries. "Lets go back, we will never make Newquay in this gale," said my companions with mounting apprehension. Ever the optimist I said " We will go on, once we get round Berry's Point, Griffin's Point and Stem Point, we will be sheltered on Watergate Beach." What I hadn't reckoned on was the fact that one cannot walk the long sweep of Watergate Beach at high tide. We either had to retrace our steps or take the cliff top path 200 feet above the 2 mile long beach. I ate humble pie and continued to lead my flagging companions. As the day wore on the storm did abate somewhat and not wishing to miss anything we walked out to Trevelgue Head. This impressive cliff castle has six ramparts and ditches and was occupied from 2000 BC to Roman times. To be quite honest there wasn't much to see on the headland apart from the ocean and the view, but I usually insisted on following the path religiously and not taking short cuts.

Back to Whipsiderry and down some stone steps to a sandy cove, sheltered by high, vertical cliffs. What a relief to get out of the wind for a while. We walked the sea front of Newquay past the hotels, guest houses and the B & B's almost all displaying vacancy signs at this time of year or closed completely. The place was dead, all their owners waiting patiently for the brief summer season. We continued right out to the tip of Towan Head, around Fistral Beach to Pentire Point East then back alongside Crantock Beach as far as the ferry crossing. The River Gannel is tidal at this point and impassable to walkers. We managed to catch a bus back to Mawgan Porth, it had been a long, tiresome walk, most of the time leaning into the wind. We would solve the problem of crossing the Gannel after a hearty meal and a good nights sleep!

26th April 1994
West bank of the Gannel to Perranporth – 10 miles

To continue our walk of the North Cornish coastline we had to find somewhere to stay on the western side of the Gannel estuary. No great problem early in the holiday season especially in an area where every third house offers accommodation. At least that is what we thought. In Newquay and the surrounding district it would have been no problem, but the village of Crantock where we hoped to stay is isolated and off the beaten track. B & B signs with vacancies were sparse. By now the best of the day had gone and it was beginning to look like we would have to spend a night in the car or drive back to Newquay and sojourn at some expensive hotel where the guests dressed for dinner and talked with a plum in their mouth. A trio of wind shattered hikers who smelt of sea weed and saltwater wouldn't be welcomed with open arms!

The village of Crantock has a touch of 'old world' charm boasting a small shop, a thatched pub and a delightful church, famous for superior carvings and its stocks. In desperation Ruth said, "The shop isn't shut yet, I'll pop in and ask if they can recommend a B & B close by." Minutes later my wife came out of the shop all smiles. "There is just a chance Crantock Plains Farmhouse can offer us accommodation, apparently it is only a couple of miles up the road." And that is how we stumbled upon Buzz and Jackie Rowlands who in my opinion run the best B & B in Cornwall. They have a delightful house, cosy and inviting, dating back 250 years, where log fires on chilly evenings enhanced our stay in the days that followed. Another big plus for us was the fact that Buzz offered to act as unpaid chauffeur collecting us from the end of each days walk even though it did eventually mean a round trip of fifty miles or more. After a good nights sleep and an excellent 'English Breakfast' we were on our way by 9.30 am following the west bank of the River Gannel and making for Crantock Beach. Our hosts hearing of our planned walk warned us that in places the path runs close to some sheer drops, and if a strong wind is blowing, particularly an easterly, it might be wiser to chose an inland route. Initially it proved to be easy walking through riverside meadows a patchwork of cowslips, bluebells, primroses, violets and wild white garlic. On reaching Crantock Beach at the seaward end of the River Gannel's estuary we made our way through high and extensive dunes which back onto a broad expanse of low-tide sand. It can be a long drag on foot around Pentire Point West so to be honest we cheated and took a short cut across the peninsular to reach Porth Joke, locally known as Polly Joke. This attractive little bay, owned by The National Trust, nestles between low cliffs whose rocks give way to gently sloping headlands, patchworked with small fields lightly stocked with cattle and sheep and obviously farmed on 'the dog and stick' principal. We didn't cheat on the next big headland, but marched all the way out to Kelsey Head perhaps as much as anything to get a good view of 'The Chick' a small rocky island where seals are known to breed. Now followed a very tortuous route as the path clings to the cliff top all the way to Holywell Beach. Having by now walked almost 600 miles of the South West Way Ruth and I have learnt the hard way that Britain's coastline is hundreds of miles long, and immensely varied. In some places, towering cliffs and jagged rocks provide a mighty bulwark against the huge seas that crash against the coast. At other spots waves lap gently upon sandy beaches in sheltered coves, each of these different habitats harbour its own range and individual species of wildlife uniquely adapted to life by the sea. At hundreds of places all around the coast, rugged headlands thrust out into the sea and in the turbulent waters around these headlands, strong, dangerous currents swirl, an ever present danger to small boats and unsuspecting swimmers. The birds which nest on the cliffs are mostly fish eaters, exploiting the marine life which flourishes in the sea below, whilst on the beach raucous gull cries fill the air. Right down to the tideline the clockwork scurry of sanderlings hunt sandhoppers just ahead of the incoming tide. To see nature at its best it is advisable to get there early in the morning or out of season as the wildlife evaporates with the onrush of trippers, deckchairs, dogs and damp children.

Reaching the western end of Holywell Beach we had to ford the broad but shallow river which meanders seawards. At the expense of very wet feet I managed to scramble across on some well placed stepping stones. Sensible Delcie and Ruth took off their boots and socks to wade across without mishap. Ahead of us now towered the massive 300 foot high cliff of Penhale Point, dangerous disused mine shafts and for good measure the obstacle of Penhale Army Camp. Prominent red signs emphasise the need for walkers to keep to the path, avoid any short cuts, and obey sentries posted on the rifle range. The wild cliff scenery of this area is unbelievable, inaccessible Hoblyn's Cove, and wind battered Ligger Point, to name but two. There are no roads, no houses, no farms with the whole coastline guarded by the vast danger area of Penhale Army Camp. When we did finally reach Perran Beach our luck was in for once. With the tide out and the booming surf just a distant murmur we could walk the three mile stretch of golden sand to Perranporth, but to do this first we had to descend an almost vertical cliff face, the alternative was to follow the monotonous path through the sand dunes at the rear of the beach. We chose the foremost a foolhardy decision that could easily have lead to serious injury if either of us had slipped, we were fully equipped for hiking but not for abseiling rocky cliffs. Needless to say I wouldn't be writing this narrative if we hadn't made a safe descent. After walking and climbing for eight hours we reached the popular and compact little holiday resort of Perranporth. Waiting for us as previously arranged was our host Buzz Rowlands eager to transport us back to Crantock Plains House where a three course meal awaited our return.

27th April 1994
Perranporth to Porthtowan – 8 miles

The 27th April 1994 was a mild spring day but as usual in the west country a gale blew in off the Atlantic. It seems like the wind never stops blowing in Cornwall, no wonder all the stunted trees on the coast lean with the prevailing wind.

After an early morning drive to Perranporth we parked our car in the car park at the back of the beach it was the only vehicle there except for an optimistic ice cream salesman in a Mr Whippy van. Come July / August the place will be chock-a-block with cars and people by 10 am. We resisted the temptation to be the ice cream man's first customers of the day and set off following the road which climbs upwards along the south side of Perran Beach. It is the start of some fine cliff walking through what used to be a flourishing copper and tin mining area. I had estimated that Porthtowan was about four miles ahead but in fact I had miscalculated the distance due to the fact that a small corner of the coastline in this area is shown in the top left hand corner of the O. S. map number 203 which unfortunately we didn't have with us. A simple mistake that was to add some 4 miles to our planned walk

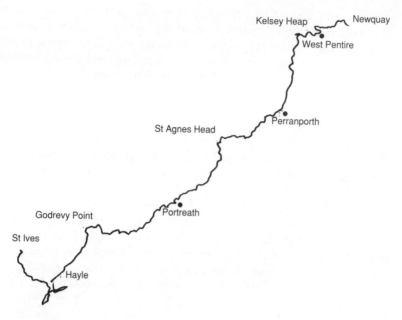

for the day. No wonder it took us 7 hours with just one refreshment break at Trevaunance Cove. An amusing incident occurred on this particular walk, whilst negotiating the area known as the Blue Hill, I had just pointed out to my two companions the fact that we had not seen or met another person in three days of walking when around a huge crag came at least thirty helmeted geologists making for a nearby quarry to study rock formations. They seemed as surprised to see us as we were to see them! As we approached St. Agnes Head the path skirted the very edge of the cliff top, most dangerous in places. Ruth was not too happy walking this very narrow path with sheer drops to the waves below. The views from this point are staggering, nearly 30 miles of coast line can be seen on a clear day. The walk then developed into a high level trail as we struck off the next few miles to Chapel Porth a lonely, isolated cove, and a secret haunt for summer holiday makers in the know. We had been told that we would find a tea shop there. The vision of a pot of tea and perhaps partaking in a hot Cornish pasty in a cosy cafe kept us going. But oh, what a disappointment to find the place completely deserted and the shop windows boarded up. To console ourselves we sat on a stone wall, watched the huge waves roll in and ate a chocolate bar each. Two hours later we reached Porthtowan.

28th April 1994
Porthtowan to Portreath and beyond, to Northcliff. Then continuing as far as the 4th car park off the B3301 – 4 miles

Now if this piece of navigational information seems rather precise it was because at this point the B3301 comes within 30 yards or so of the South West Coastal Path. It was at this particular pick up point that we arranged to meet our helpful friend Buzz Rolands at 5pm. Today we would be keeping to a strict timetable, no diversions from the path to view some ruin or ancient church, no lingering visit to some quiet cove. We resolved not to waste time looking for seals in the sea below and would limit the number of refreshment stops.

It was a stiff climb up from Porthtowan beach but once on the cliff-top we were rewarded by our first view of St Ives Head some 20 miles west, our final objective. The cliffs drop sheer some 250 feet to the sea as we passed high above the little headland Tobban Horse. Just south west of here the Royal Engineers have built steps on either side of the very steep Sally's Bottom. We had this amusingly named little cove to ourselves except for the sea birds and the seals. As we scrambled up the other side, the path hugs the security fence of the Nancekuke Defence Establishment. Whilst this section is not very scenic at least it is level allowing us to make good time. When we did eventually reach Portreath we sat on the sea front and enjoyed an ice cream-a treat I allowed my two companions and myself as we had made such good time. On our previous four days of walking we had resisted the temptation. We had long discovered that such luxury doesn't mix with steep cliff climbs. After allowing ourselves just 30 minutes recuperation we moved out of Portreath on the narrow country road south of the harbour. This leads past some houses to a footpath climbing continuously through a green valley and round Western Hill to the cliff top. We were still only approximately halfway to the arranged rendezvous with Buzz and the guide book reports, "Path strenuous in parts with many ups and downs," I was in the lead and realised we must get a move on so I started to take longer strides leaving my companions bewailing somewhat. "Hey Bertus, what's the great rush all of a sudden," shouted my sister. "If we knock off a few miles I'll allow a lunch break in a bit," I replied blithely. It worked, like offering a carrot to a donkey.

Once more we had the coast line to ourselves rounding every headland, exploring every combe the view is different, no two areas the same. Lots of small, rocky islands just off shore on this section. Gull Rock, Horse Rock, Samphire Island, Ralph's Cupboard, and the Crane Islands, to name but a few. By 3pm we had reached Basset's Cove a beautiful spot, sheltered by high cliffs. We had been so engrossed in the scenery that only now did we realise how hungry we were having had nothing to eat since an early breakfast, except for the ice cream of course. Our kind landlady by special request had made some bacon butties for our midday lunch break. Sitting on rocks with the waves lapping at our bare toes, in eager anticipation we unwrapped our individual packs. What a disappointment we had. The good lady had carefully tin foil wrapped some well fried bacon assuming that we would be carrying some sliced bread and some butter-of course we had neither! Fortunately whilst in Portreath we had purchased a jam doughnut each which was some consolation. Just another amusing incident on our travels but we didn't laugh at the time.

We reached the 4th car park 5 minutes early, just as Buzz pulled in, what timing. Later that evening we dined at the Old Albion in Crantock village on rather better fare than fried bacon and a doughnut.

29th April 1994
From the 4th Car Park west on High Cliff to St Ives – 16 miles

All the weather signs in my book forecast a fine dry day. Clear, sparkling skies with just a light breeze blowing offshore. The sort of weather when one feels on top of the world. Well later we would be on some very high cliffs, maybe not quite on top of the world but much less dangerous than on some snow-capped mountain in the Himalayas. We were now some 25 miles from Crantock Plains Farmhouse to our intended starting point for the day. We couldn't expect Buzz to do a 50 mile round trip on our behalf so we drove our own car. It was 10 am when we started walking westward on what, for Ruth and me, was the last lap of our coastal path marathon. On the exposed North Cliff a path running seaward off the road has been cut through dense scrub and gorse. It twists and turns but otherwise it proved to be easy walking. Further along is Hudder Cove where far below are the remains of the Cecil Japan, this ship, wrecked in March 1989 with all but one of the crew saved by helicopter. Apparently the one seaman lost had panicked, jumped into the sea and drowned. It took us some while to determine which way the wreck lay, on its side or bow uppermost so damaged are the remains. Even after a prolonged debate we were not completely sure. Just beyond this spot one comes to an awe inspiring cleft in the coastline "Hells Mouth" where an inadequate wooden fence guards a spectacular drop to the beach, the site of many suicides-I am given to understand. Turning sharply northwest the path leads to Navax Point where we stopped for our first break of the day. It is an excellent spot for observing sea birds. Far from the activities of man they were there in large numbers, fulmers, sea gulls, gannets and shearwaters, whilst in the caves below the Point are breeding places for the grey seals. The cliff faces themselves were a riot of colour, bluebells, primroses, spring squills. Truly a wondrous spot to share with nature.

Another mile or so and we were at Godrevy Point where low cliffs rise above flat rocks, dappled with low tide pools. Savage rocks check the path of the racing tide and churn the sea to flying spume. Between The Point and Godrevy Island lie wicked looking rocks that have claimed many ships before the lighthouse was built in 1859. As we moved on we realised that we had now conquered the last great headland on our long march around the south west coast of England. Ruth and I had stood on the point of each and every one. I suppose we felt like the mountaineer with no more peaks to challenge. Rather sad in a way, but I wouldn't wish to do it all again. Across the bay, a grey shimmer in the distance was St. Ives Head, now partly hidden by a sea mist. Down hill all the way now, at least that is what we told ourselves, we needed some encouragement to keep our legs going those last few miles.

In front of us now stretched four miles of golden sand, one of the longest beaches in Cornwall. But to reach it, first we had to ford the Red River which crosses the beach on the eastern side. We seemed to have learnt nothing from our previous experience of crossing rivers. This time all three of us attempted to cross on algae covered stepping stones only to slip into the water and get very wet indeed. Once safely on the other side we removed our boots and socks, something we should have done before attempting the crossing. Walking across the sand some distance back from the sea, perhaps the most noticeable feature on the beach is the storm ridge, a line of pebbles thrown up parallel to the sea by storm tides. Only occasionally does the sea reach this far up the beach. The strand line-that unlovely mix of rotting seaweed, plastic bottles and other flotsam. On and on across this sweeping expanse of sea washed sand, our destination, Black Cliff. It didn't seem to get any closer. Legs still willing but heart and lungs protesting. Heading into a gathering wind, short of breath and very weary. Don't give up now I tell myself not on the last ten miles. "What have we got left to eat?" I enquired of my companions." Just one bar of chocolate and an orange, no more drink left, the water bottles are empty, I am told. We all flopped down on the damp sand and ate the last of our rations. After a short break moved on again, 1760 yards to the mile, how many strides I wonder. Over halfway across the beach by now. Finally we reached the rundown harbour of Hayle. Some entrepreneur, whose name I won't mention hopes to raise 250 million pounds to rejuvenate the place. It will be good news for the area if improvements do go ahead. There is no longer a ferry service across the estuary which is bad news for walkers making for St Ives as it adds four or five miles to one's journey. We made for the old swing bridge over Carnsew Pool, then followed the road around the inlet, under the railway viaduct until reaching the causeway. Walking the pavement alongside this busy road was an unpleasant experience. The whiz, whiz of late afternoon traffic was terrible, such a contrast to the lonely, uninhabited clifftops and isolated coves we had got so use to. For a while I tried thumbing a lift to St Ives but no vehicle stopped. Perhaps to the drivers we gave the appearance of three 'New Age Travellers', dropouts best left to our own devices. Once across The Causeway the main road continues westwards but at 'Old Quay House Inn' the official path swings right keeping to a lane which in due course leads to the church of St Uny. Leaving the churchyard on the right the path crosses a golf course, dips under a very low bridge before keeping alongside the railway line. Now well above Porth Kidney Sands. "How much further," I was repeatedly asked. "Just another mile or two." "You have been saying that for the last ten miles," my sister reminded me crossly. "OK we will take a 20 minute break." No one needed to be told twice. We laid flat out amongst the sand dunes but unfortunately the respite was short-lived; myriads of ants forced us to make a hasty retreat. This section was one of the longest we had attempted, somehow we had to keep going.

It was 7 pm when we arrived at the bus station in St Ives. To my inquiry the answer was. "There are no more buses to Portreath today but I can get you a taxi." One was with us in three minutes. How's that for service?!

Ruth and I had walked the whole length of the South West Coastal Path. 594 miles in 74 days an average of 8.02 miles per day.

To summarise:-
In my memories are the everlasting cliff climbs, climbing up and up then when one finally staggers to the top the path drops again often to sea level, before one must clamber upwards yet again. And so it goes on, yet I wouldn't wish to give the impression that I'm not pleased to have conquered this pathway. I did at one point

St. Ives

calculate that if one could stand the path upright it would be 108 times higher than Mount Everest's 29,002 feet summit. But then it wasn't all up hill some was downhill and of course not nearly so cold! I often put the question to myself. "Why are you doing this walk?" It cannot be to prove anything, many others have done it. Well, yes maybe they have but perhaps not too many with a dodgey ticker and who has already enjoyed 70 years on this planet. I guess I should have got myself sponsored giving the money to some charity.

Another plus for Ruth and me, having now completed this walk from Poole to Minehead is that we do know the whereabouts of Hope's Nose, Start Point, Bolt's Head or Dorset's Golden Cap. That Cape Cornwall is more to our liking than Land's End. That there is a Blackpool Beach on the south coast and we do know The Great Hangman from The Little Hangman. We had arrived footsore and travel-soiled yet elated. This walk hadn't been a bed of roses, it hadn't been easy going, there had been times when the gods had thrown everything at us in the way of hailstorms, thunderstorms, furious winds, driving rain or glaring sunshine. We'd had to grin and bear it, buckle down and head into many a south-westerly straight off the Atlantic. The years certainly were not on our side, however the main thing was:

We'd done it!